PREFACE

This book is dedicated to the memory of my parents who were responsible for introducing me to this amazing game.

INTRODUCTION

Aha! So you think you're a budding expert eh?! Well, if you've read my first book, *Bridge with Brunner – Acol Bidding for Improvers*, there is no doubting that you are!

Having resolved never to write another book on bridge (my first one was very hard work!), here I am beavering away again on my PC! Why? Have I been offered a million pounds by Batsford for a sequel? Have thousands of satisfied pupils inundated me with letters begging for more? Am I a masochist? Well, you can forget the first possibility! To be honest, the reason is purely and simply because while I am perfectly satisfied with my opening gambit in the world of writing, there is some unfinished business I have to attend to. If you have read *Bridge with Brunner – Acol Bidding for Improvers*, I feel certain that I have whetted your appetite. There is, of course, plenty more learning to come. I have never once mentioned anything on the play of the cards, or even how to defend against the opponents' final contract – but you'll have to wait a bit longer for both of those books (unless perhaps a million pounds lands on my doorstep in the very near future!).

I have already covered the basic groundwork to help you master the Acol system. Your foundations should be solid. Now, you are ready for the transition into the world of bridge on a more formal basis. The time has come for you to hone your skills and complement the structure of your system with some furnishings. Some of the topics I am covering here will just be an expansion of themes to which I made reference in *Improvers*. However, there is also a great need to incorporate some very worthwhile conventions into your repertoire – not only to help you fight fire with fire, but also, as is the case with Stayman and Fourth-suit Forcing, to provide you with an essential part of any good bridge player's weaponry. Good Luck and enjoy yourselves!

Thanks must, once again, go to John Holland and Kevin Comrie who have given me the time and space to pursue my new-found talent. To all those who have bought my first book, and are now brave enough to buy this sequel . . . heartfelt thanks, indeed. I hope I have brought a little happiness into your bridge-playing lives.

'Keep It Simple' should be any bridge player's motto. But, if you are entering the cut-throat world of competitive bridge, simplicity may not get you the desired results. In an attempt to compromise, it is my intention to introduce you to a number of treatments, variations of Acol and some 'must have in your repertoire' conventions and gadgets that will not only enable you to keep your system reasonably simple, but will also be relatively easy for you and your partner to remember. Stayman, Blackwood and Fourth-suit Forcing are but three conventions that are deemed necessary even for a beginner and, as such, were covered in my previous book. Other nuances to enhance the Acol system, to which I also made reference in *Improvers*, were Directional Asking bids (DABS) and Trial Bids. These two areas need to be addressed more fully and I have now done this for you.

At this point you may be wondering whether this book is going to be for you. "Am I really a budding expert?" you ask yourself. Well, if you didn't have any ambition to progress, you wouldn't be fingering this copy now! But there is no need to panic, because you don't have to read every single chapter to derive any benefit. They are individually wrapped so you can pick out the areas you want to explore – and as for the bits you are not yet ready to tackle . . . well, there's no sell-by date to worry about, so take your time!

I am going to present you with a concoction of worthwhile additions to your system but I cannot guarantee you perfection in your bidding. No-one can do that! Your own personal style and taste will dictate your approach to the game, and that means you have my permission to disagree with everything I have written. Feel free to go your own way. All I want to do is give you an idea of what you should be looking for if you want to up-date your current methods.

This is an easy-to-view book with the conventions and treatments tabulated for quick reference, followed by plenty of examples.

The treatments illustrated reflect the author's personal preferences but remember, there are many variations on the market. There are also hundreds more conventions that may be equally useful and even more exciting, but reading a book *that* big could put you off playing bridge for life! At the end of the day, we could all manage quite well without 90% of them. Having said that, the game would be rather dull and uninspiring without at least some of them, so here are some of them!

Come what may, I have every confidence that you will not be daunted by the contents, so sit back, have a drink and enjoy this read.

Michelle Brunner 2003

CONTENTS

Section One: Basic System

Section Two: Conventions

Section Three: Treatments

Section Four: Etiquette

Key

HCP =	High-Card Points
* =	Artificial bid and alertable
( ) =	Opponents' bids are bracketed
Dbl =	Double

SECTION ONE

BASIC SYSTEM

CHAPTER ONE

WEAK TWO OPENING BIDS
IN THREE SUITS

I have rather an amusing anecdote concerning my original intention to recommend Benjaminised Acol to you. In October 2001 I was playing in the Women's World Championships in Paris when a very eminent gentleman came to watch at our table. Sitting behind my partner, Rhona Goldenfield, he enquired as to what basic system we played. Her answer should have been Acol with weak twos in diamonds, hearts and spades. Recognising our kibbitzer as the famous Albert Benjamin of Scotland, she did not wish to offend the inventor of Benjaminised Acol and in her attempt to flatter him said we played his system. In his broad Scottish accent he retorted "Och! that's rubbish, you want to play a weak two in diamonds!" Say nay mair Albert, say nay mair!

Despite my strong conviction that the whole world should play weak two opening bids of some description, I still teach beginners the traditional Acol version of strong twos. Why? Probably because that was the route I took, so I thought – what's good enough for me . . . But, on a more serious note, I think that understanding the problems associated with expressing an 'old-fashioned' two opener can only be appreciated if you have actually played them. That's my excuse, anyway, and I'm sticking to it!

Choosing to play a system that incorporates three weak twos means that you have only one strong bid available to show a big hand. Exponents of any Strong Club system or, indeed, Benjaminised Acol will probably be reeling in the aisles at the thought. I am not moved. As far as I'm concerned, this modified version of Acol has survived the test to-date more than adequately.

As before, the 2♣ opening bid takes care of the game-forcing rock-crushers and balanced hands in the 23+ HCP range. It's just those pesky eight playing-trick hands that don't fit in anywhere now. With those, you will have to decide whether to risk making an opening bid at the one level – hoping for another chance to bid – or overstate the hand with a 2♣ opener. Personally I prefer the former as the modern trend of frisky overcalling frequently comes to my rescue!

If my argument for changing your methods seems to be full of holes, you only have to recall the number of times you actually pick up one of those big hand-types as opener. Not, I believe, often enough to worry about an occasional disaster.

Weak twos have not just got me many excellent results at the bridge table. I also get quite a buzz out of using them and deriving pleasure from the game of bridge must surely be one of the reasons we all play it! Whilst the pre-emptive style of these opening bids is intended to thwart your opponents' plans, your partnership will still be able to maintain an element of construction to the auction should the hand actually belong to your side. The only aspect of your game that now stands between victory or being vanquished is discipline. What's new there, then?

A few words of advice before launching . . .

Weak Twos are fun to play and are primarily used as a destructive weapon against your opponents. They pre-empt the bidding early and make it difficult for the opponents to find their fit and their level – especially if the bidding proceeds something like 2♠ – Pass – 4♠ – ? Quite often, however, it will be *your* side who will be pre-empted out of the best contract and, therefore, it is not the best system for accurate constructive bidding. Pick your moments cautiously – especially if you are in first or second position.

Weak Two Opening Bids in Three Suits

WEAK TWO OPENING BIDS IN THREE SUITS SYSTEM

2♣*   ACOL. 23+ HCP or 9+ playing tricks. Game forcing except for the sequence *2♣*-2◊*-2NT.*

2◊* / 2♡* / 2♠*   5-9 HCP. Non-Vulnerable. 6 card suit.
6-10 HCP. Vulnerable. 6 card suit.

---

1. RESPONSES to 2◊* / 2♡* / 2♠*:

2NT*   16+ HCP and enquires whether opener is minimum or maximum *(see next page for opener's responses to this enquiry).*

Raise to the 3 level*   To play (alertable). It is a pre-emptive manoeuvre with 3-card support and between 9-15 HCP. *Not* invitational.

New suit at the 2 level   Non-forcing but constructive. Opener's choices include raising with a suitable hand, passing without, or rebidding own suit.

New suit at the 3 level   Natural and forcing for one round. Raise with 3 trumps or a doubleton honour.

New suit at the 4 level*   Splinter bid. This cue-bid agrees the opening suit as trumps, and shows slam interest with a singleton or void in the bid suit *(see Chapter 9 on Splinters).* **N.B.** Watch out for the auctions: 2♠ – 4♡, and 2♡ – 4♠.

Raises to game   To play. The hand may be weak or strong depending on how many trumps responder holds. In this respect, the element of surprise awaits both opener and opponents alike!

WEAK TWO OPENING BIDS IN THREE SUITS
SYSTEM CONTINUED

2◇* – 4◇	A pre-emptive manoeuvre and *not* invitational.

2. OPENER'S RESPONSE TO THE 2NT ENQUIRY
   (game-invitational+)

Rebid of suit opened*
Minimum.
5-7 Not Vulnerable, 6-8 Vulnerable.

New suit* *non-jump*
Maximum.
8-9 Not Vulnerable, 9-10 Vulnerable.
(This 'suit' merely shows a high-card feature, i.e. ace, king or queen and may be just two cards in length.)

Rebid of 3NT*
Very good suit headed by the ace.
e.g. A-K-Q-x-x-x, A-K-J-x-x-x, A-Q-J-x-x-x.
(With a singleton you should prefer to Splinter.)

Jump in a new suit*
Maximum and a Splinter in bid suit.

GENERAL PRINCIPLES
AND DISCUSSION POINTS

1. Holding four or more trumps in support, you should raise partner's weak two opener to the four level often, regardless of strength, and especially if the vulnerability is favourable.

2. Define your expectation of suit quality at each vulnerability. I recommend that your suit is headed by one of the top three honours if vulnerable.

3. Discuss whether you may have another 4-card suit when opening with a weak two – or even the other major!

4. Opening a weak two with a ropy 7-card suit is not out of the question. There must have been many occasions when you were itching to open with a three-level pre-empt but knew it would be imprudent – perhaps owing to the poor quality of your suit or the unfavourable vulnerability. Well, now's your chance to get in on the action, albeit a level lower.

5. In all cases, continuations by the 2NT bidder are forcing to game.

6. In fourth seat you should revert to Acol Two opening bids. Now, I knew there was a good reason for knowing how to play them!

1. *What would you open first-in-hand non-vulnerable?*

Hand 1a	**Hand 1b**	**Hand 1c**
♠ 6 5	♠ A Q 6 5 4 3	♠ K J 9
♡ K Q 6 5 4 3	♡ 9 8	♡ 8 7
◇ 2	◇ 9 8 6	◇ Q 8 7 6 5 4
♣ 7 6 5 4	♣ 8 3	♣ 3 2
5 HCP	6 HCP	6 HCP

Hand 1d	**Hand 1e**	**Hand 1f**
♠ 8 7 6	♠ 9 8 7	♠ K J 5 4 3 2
♡ Q J 9 6 5 4	♡ 6 5 4	♡ A 4 3
◇ A 2	◇ A K J 8 7 6	◇ J 5 3
♣ 6 5	♣ 4	♣ 4
7 HCP	8 HCP	9 HCP

2. *How about vulnerable?*

Hand 2a	**Hand 2b**	**Hand 2c**
♠ Q 8 7 6 5 4	♠ 4 3 2	♠ K 3
♡ Q 2	♡ J 8 7 6 5 4	♡ 2
◇ 6 4 3	◇ A J	◇ Q J 9 8 6 5 4
♣ J 8 4	♣ 8 3	♣ J 5 4
5 HCP	6 HCP	7 HCP

Hand 2d	**Hand 2e**	**Hand 2f**
♠ A K J 7 5 2	♠ 9	♠ K
♡ 5 4	♡ Q 9 7 5 4 3	♡ A J 8 7 6 5
◇ 8 7 6	◇ A K 2	◇ Q 5 3 2
♣ 7 2	♣ 7 5 3	♣ 8 3
8 HCP	9 HCP	10 HCP

Continued on next page – Answers on page 18

3. *Your partner opens with a weak 2♡ first in hand non-vulnerable.*
   Your right-hand opponent passes. How would you respond?

Hand 3a	**Hand 3b**	**Hand 3c**
♠ A 4	♠ K Q 9 5	♠ K J 7
♡ Q 9 8 7	♡ A 9 8 5	♡ K 7 3
◊ 9	◊ K 5 4	◊ A Q 3 2
♣ J 8 7 6 5 2	♣ 3 2	♣ 8 6 3
7 HCP	12 HCP	13 HCP

Hand 3d	**Hand 3e**	**Hand 3f**
♠ Q J 7 5	♠ A J 7	♠ A K
♡ J 3	♡ J 7 6 3	♡ Q J 8 2
◊ Q J 7 4	◊ A K J 7	◊ A 8 4
♣ A K Q	♣ K 4	♣ A 7 6 5
16 HCP	17 HCP	18 HCP

4. *Your partner opens with a weak 2◊ first in hand vulnerable.*
   Your right-hand opponent passes. How would you respond?

Hand 4a	**Hand 4b**	**Hand 4c**
♠ 5	♠ 8 7 6	♠ K J 7 2
♡ Q 9 8 6 3	♡ K Q 6 5	♡ A K Q 7 6
◊ K Q 8 7 6	◊ Q J 7	◊ 3
♣ 6 5	♣ 9 8 2	♣ Q 6 3
7 HCP	8 HCP	15 HCP

Hand 4d	**Hand 4e**	**Hand 4f**
♠ K Q J 5	♠ A J 9 8 7 6	♠ A J 6
♡ Q J 7 2	♡ A 7	♡ K Q 3 2
◊ 3	◊ J 2	◊ K Q 2
♣ A Q J 2	♣ A K 2	♣ K Q 2
16 HCP	17 HCP	20 HCP

Answers on page 18

1a	1b	1c
2♡*	2♠*	2♢*

1d	1e	1f
2♡*	2♢*	2♠*

2a	2b	2c
Pass	Pass	2♢*

2d	2e	2f
2♠*	2♡*	2♡*

3a	3b	3c
4♡	4♡	3♡*

3d	3e	3f
2NT*	4♡	4♡

4a	4b	4c
4♢	3♢*	2♡

4d	4e	4f
2NT*	3♠	3NT

DEFENCE TO WEAK TWOS SYSTEM

Double

TAKE-OUT; either: (a) 13+ HCP shortage in suit opened and support for the other three suits, or (b) 19+ HCP. Too strong for 2NT.

♠ 2	♠ K J 5
♡ A K 6 5	♡ A Q 8
◇ K J 4 2	◇ K Q J 2
♣ Q 9 8 3	♣ A J 6
(2♠*) – Dbl	(2♡*) – Dbl

Two-level overcall

5+ card suit. 13+ HCP or extra shape.

♠ A Q J 7 5	♠ A 4
♡ 8 2	♡ K J 8 7 5 3
◇ K 6 5 3	◇ 4 3
♣ A 4	♣ K J 7
(2♡*) – 2♠	(2◇*) – 2♡

2NT

15-18 HCP balanced and a stopper in the bid suit. Responses as over a 2NT opener.

♠ K 7 6	♠ Q J 8
♡ A J 3	♡ K Q 4
◇ Q 9 8	◇ A Q 8 6 4
♣ A K 5 4	♣ Q 3
(2♠*) – 2NT	(2♡*) – 2NT

DEFENCE TO WEAK TWOS
SYSTEM CONTINUED

Three-level overcall
Non-jump

Approx. 12-15 HCP. 6+ card suit or two-suited. *(May be slightly stronger when a jump bid entails bidding at the four level.)* Non-forcing.

♠ 7 6	♠ 5
♡ K 4 2	♡ A K Q 5 4
◇ A K J 8 7 3	◇ Q 7
♣ A 9	♣ K Q 8 7 6
(2♡*) – 3◇	(2♠*) – 3♡

Three-level overcall
Jump bid

Strong. Approx. 16-19 HCP. Good suit. Non-forcing.

♠ A Q J 5 4 3	♠ Q J
♡ K 7 2	♡ K Q J 7 6 5
◇ K Q 4	◇ A K
♣ J	♣ Q 4 2
(2♡*) – 3♠	(2◇*) – 3♡

3◇* 3♡* 3♠*
Cue-bid of the opponent's suit

Requesting stop in opponent's suit for no-trumps. Game values. Suggests long strong suit.

♠ K 5	♠ Q 5
♡ 4 3	♡ A K
◇ A K Q J 5 4 3	◇ 3 2
♣ A 2	♣ A K Q J 9 8 7
(2♡*) – 3♡*	(2◇*) – 3◇*

DEFENCE TO WEAK TWOS
SYSTEM CONTINUED

3NT

To play. A source of tricks and a stopper in the opponent's suit.

♠ A 4	♠ J 8
♡ K	♡ A Q
◇ A K Q 9 8 7 4	◇ Q 2
♣ Q 3 2	♣ A K J 8 7 6 5

(2♠*) – 3NT   (2♡*) – 3NT

4♣* / 4◇*
over 2♡ or 2♠**

Leaping Michaels.
5+ cards in bid minor and 5+ cards in unbid major. Game values.

♠ A K J 5 4	♠ 2
♡ 9 2	♡ K Q J 5 2
◇ A K Q J 3	◇ A 4
♣ 8	♣ A Q J 6 5

(2♡*) – 4◇*   (2♠*) – 4♣*

4♣*
*over 2◇**

Leaping Michaels.
5+ clubs and a 5-card major.
Game values.

♠ A Q J 6 5	♠ —
♡ 2	♡ A K 8 7 6
◇ 8 7	◇ K J 3
♣ A K Q 5 4	♣ K Q J 6 5

(2◇) – 4♣*   (2◇) – 4♣*

DEFENCE TO WEAK TWOS
SYSTEM CONTINUED

4◇*
*over 2◇**

Both majors and a good hand. At least 5-5.

♠ A K Q 7 6   ♠ K Q J 7 6
♡ A K Q J 4   ♡ A Q J 5 4 3
◇ 4 3   ◇ 2
♣ 2   ♣ 7

(2◇*) – 4◇*   (2◇*) – 4◇*

4♡ / 4♠

Game values. Good 6+ card suit.

♠ K Q J 9 7 6 4   ♠ K Q 2
♡ 3   ♡ A Q J 8 6 4 2
◇ A 6   ◇ 2
♣ K Q 3   ♣ A Q

(2♡*) – 4♠   (2◇*) – 4♡

4NT*
over 2♡ or 2♠**

Unusual No-trump.
At least 5-5 in the minors.
Strong or very shapely.

♠ 3   ♠ 6
♡ 8 2   ♡ 9
◇ A K Q 7 3   ◇ K Q J 5 4 2
♣ A K Q 8 2   ♣ A K J 8 4

(2♡*) – 4NT*   (2♠*) – 4NT*

DEFENCE TO WEAK TWOS
SYSTEM CONTINUED

Protective Double
(4th seat)

Take-out ; either: (a) 11+ HCP, shortage in suit opened and support for the other three suits, or: (b) 19+ HCP. Too strong for 2NT.

♠ K J 5 4
♡ 2
◊ Q 8 6 4
♣ K Q 6 5

(2♡*) – Pass – (Pass) – Dbl

♠ A K 7
♡ A J 6
◊ A Q 5 4
♣ Q 3 2

(2♠*) – Pass – (Pass) – Dbl

GENERAL PRINCIPLES
AND DISCUSSION POINTS

1. The simplest form of defence is to treat the weak two opening bid as a one-level opener: i.e. double for take-out and overcall 2NT to show 15-18 HCP. However, with borderline decisions the prevailing vulnerability should play a large part in determining whether or not to bid, as you are at a higher level.

2. If one opponent opens with a weak two and the other raises this suit pre-emptively to the three level after your partner makes a take-out double, you can show that you have some values by doubling this contract. It is not a penalty double based on trumps, rather it is more inclined for take-out. e.g. (2♡*) – Dbl – (3♡) – Dbl might look like:

    ♠ K65
    ♡ A2
    ♢ Q654
    ♣ Q543

    Similarly, a double after a raise to the four level will also be based on general values, e.g. (2♠*) – Dbl – (4♠) – Dbl might be made holding:

    ♠ K5
    ♡ J54
    ♢ A7652
    ♣ Q43

    If you want to force partner to pick a suit, you can use the 4NT bid to express a distributional two-suited hand, e.g.

    ♠ A4
    ♡ 2
    ♢ KJ654
    ♣ Q9876

1. *Your right-hand opponent opens 2◇ weak. What would you overcall?*

Hand 1a
♠ K J 8 7 3 2
♡ K 3
◇ A J 8 6
♣ 3

12 HCP

Hand 1b
♠ A J 6 5
♡ K Q 4 3
◇ 3
♣ K 6 5 4

13 HCP

Hand 1c
♠ Q 4 3
♡ A 4
◇ J 7
♣ K Q J 7 6 5

13 HCP

Hand 1d
♠ A 5 4
♡ A K Q 5 4 3
◇ K 8
♣ 4 3

16 HCP

Hand 1e
♠ K J 7
♡ A J 6 5
◇ A J 8
♣ Q 3 2

16 HCP

Hand 1f
♠ A 2
♡ Q 2
◇ K 4
♣ A K Q J 7 6 5

19 HCP

2. *Your right-hand opponent opens 2♡ weak. What would you overcall?*

Hand 2a
♠ A J 8 7 6
♡ 5 4
◇ K 8
♣ K J 5 4

12 HCP

Hand 2b
♠ 4
♡ 2
◇ A K J 7 6
♣ K Q 7 6 5 4

13 HCP

Hand 2c
♠ Q J 7 4
♡ 4
◇ A K 9 2
♣ Q J 5 3

13 HCP

Hand 2d
♠ A K J 7 6 5
♡ J 6 3
◇ A J 3
♣ 5

14 HCP

Hand 2e
♠ K 9 8
♡ Q 9 2
◇ A K Q 4 3
♣ J 7

15 HCP

Hand 2f
♠ A K J
♡ K J 7
◇ Q 4 3
♣ A J 8 7

19 HCP

Continued on next page – Answers on page 28

3. *Your right-hand opponent opens 2♠ weak. What would you overcall?*

Hand 3a
- ♠ A Q 7 6 5
- ♡ 5 4
- ◊ K 7 6 5
- ♣ A 4

13 HCP

Hand 3b
- ♠ 6
- ♡ A J 8 6
- ◊ K Q 3
- ♣ A 9 8 7 6

14 HCP

Hand 3c
- ♠ Q J
- ♡ A K
- ◊ J 7 5 4 3
- ♣ Q J 3 2

14 HCP

Hand 3d
- ♠ —
- ♡ A K 9 8 6 5 4
- ◊ A Q J 9
- ♣ J 7

15 HCP

Hand 3e
- ♠ A J 9
- ♡ Q J 5 4
- ◊ K 5 3
- ♣ A K 6

18 HCP

Hand 3f
- ♠ 4
- ♡ A K Q 9 8
- ◊ K 2
- ♣ A K J 7 5

20 HCP

4. *Your left-hand opponent opens 2♡ weak. Partner doubles.*
How would you respond?

Hand 4a
- ♠ 8 6 4 2
- ♡ 7 6 5
- ◊ 9 8 2
- ♣ 5 4 3

0 HCP

Hand 4b
- ♠ K 8 7 6
- ♡ A 3 2
- ◊ K 9 7 2
- ♣ J 2

11 HCP

Hand 4c
- ♠ Q 3 2
- ♡ A Q 9 8 7
- ◊ 8 6 2
- ♣ K 7

11 HCP

Hand 4d
- ♠ J 5 2
- ♡ A Q 8
- ◊ Q 6 3
- ♣ Q 4 3 2

11 HCP

Hand 4e
- ♠ 8 7 4
- ♡ K J 9
- ◊ A 7 6 5
- ♣ K Q 2

13 HCP

Hand 4f
- ♠ 4 3
- ♡ 7 6 5
- ◊ A K J 7
- ♣ K Q J 2

14 HCP

Answers on page 28

Defence to Weak Twos

Answers to Examples on pages 25-26

1a	1b	1c
2♠	Dbl	3♣

1d	1e	1f
3♡	2NT	3NT

2a	2b	2c
2♠	4NT*	Dbl

2d	2e	2f
2♠	2NT	Dbl

3a	3b	3c
Pass	Dbl	Pass

3d	3e	3f
4♡	2NT	4♣*

4a	4b	4c
2♠	3♠	Pass

4d	4e	4f
2NT	3NT	3♡*

SECTION TWO

CONVENTIONS

CHAPTER TWO

TRANSFERS OVER 2NT

If you are considering playing Transfers over 1NT, you might like to have a peek at this chapter first. The Transfer system over 2NT is far less daunting and reasonably simple to follow – a comparative doddle in fact – especially if you are a budding expert!

When you pick up a balanced hand with 20-22 HCP, your choice of opening bid is simple: it's 2NT. This limit bid has, to all intents and purposes, described your hand perfectly, so why do you need a sophisticated set of responses? With no system, other than Stayman, at your disposal, your options are to Pass or go marching on to game. There is no 'in-between' weak take-out bid available to you at the three level, often resulting in an unnecessary minus score and a waste of a good hand. That's a good enough answer for my money and so it's Transfers to the rescue!

One of the three main benefits to playing Transfers is to allow the contract to be literally 'transferred' to the other hand. Of course, that is not necessarily good news if your partner does not play the cards too well but, seriously, there is a definite advantage in concealing the 'big' hand from the defenders. Being able to stop in a part-score at the three level with a very weak hand has obvious merits, too. But the best reason by far lies simply in having more scope to develop the auction.

As with all changes to your system, you will need to practise them regularly. 2NT opening bids may not be all that common but there are other situations where these exact methods can be used, and three instances spring to mind at once: (1) following a protective 2NT call (19-21 HCP); (2) after a 2NT overcall in defence to a weak two opening bid (15-18 HCP); and (3) in continuation of the sequence 2♣* – 2◊* – 2NT (23-24 HCP).

While we are on the subject of up-dating your current methods in this department, it seems an appropriate time to modernise your present meaning of the 3♣ response too. As an alternative to Stayman, the Baron 3♣ convention meshes well with this version of Transfers.

TRANSFERS AND BARON 3♣*
RESPONSES TO 2NT – SYSTEM

3♣*   Baron. Asking for four-card suits in ascending order. If opener's only suit is clubs the response is 3NT.

3◇*   Transfer showing 5+ hearts. Opener is commanded to bid 3♡.

3♡*   Transfer showing 5+ spades. Opener is commanded to bid 3♠.

3♠*   Shows 5 spades and 4 hearts. Opener chooses the best game.

3NT   To play.

4♣   6+ clubs. Forcing. Slam interest. (Prefer Gerber? You choose – but consult partner!)

4◇   6+ diamonds. Forcing. Slam interest.

4♡   6+ hearts. Non-forcing. Mild slam interest. Without slam interest you should transfer to 3♡ and then raise to game.

4♠   6+ spades. Non-forcing. Mild slam interest. Without slam interest you should transfer to 3♠ and then raise to game.

4NT   Natural and quantitative, asking opener to pass with a minimum or bid 6NT with a maximum.

5NT   15-16 HCP. *Forcing!* Asks opener to bid 6NT with a minimum and 7NT with a maximum.

6NT   13-14 HCP. To play.

1.
East	West	East
♠ A J x x x x	2NT	3♡*
♡ x x	3♠*	4♠
◇ x x x		
♣ x x		

Transfer to spades and raise to show a 6+ suit and game values.

2.
East	West	East
♠ Q x	2NT	3◇*
♡ J x x x x	3♡*	3NT
◇ K x x		
♣ x x x		

A transfer to hearts followed by a 3NT rebid shows 5 hearts and offers a choice of games.

3.
East	West	East
♠ Q x x x x	2NT	3♠*
♡ A x x x	3NT	
◇ x x		
♣ x x		

Shows 5 spades and 4 hearts. Forcing to game.

4.
East	West	East
♠ K x x x x	2NT	3♡*
♡ Q x x x x	3♠*	4♡
◇ x		
♣ x x		

Shows 5-5 in the majors. Asks for preference.

5.

East	West	East
♠ A x x x	2NT	3♣*
♡ x	3♡	3♠
◇ K J x x	3NT	Pass
♣ x x x x		

Use Baron to look for a 4-4 fit.

6.

East	West	East
♠ A x x x	2NT	3♣*
♡ x	3◇	4NT*
◇ K Q J x	5♡*	6◇
♣ K x x x		

Here's another Baron sequence. A neat way to locate a diamond slam.

7.

East	West	East
♠ K x x	2NT	4♣
♡ x x		
◇ Q x		
♣ A J x x x x		

A slam try in clubs. (I'm not a Gerber fan if you've not already guessed!)

8.

East	West	East
♠ A x	2NT	4♡
♡ K J x x x x		
◇ J x x		
♣ x x		

A mild slam try in hearts. Compare with sequence 1, page 33.

9.
East	West	East
♠ K Q x x x	2NT	3♡*
♡ Q x x	3♠*	5NT*
◇ K J x		
♣ Q x		

Pick a slam in spades or no-trumps.

10.
East	West	East
♠ K x x	2NT	3◇*
♡ A x x x x	3♡*	4NT
◇ Q x x		
♣ Q x		

Quantitative with 5 hearts.

11.
East	West	East
♠ x x x x x x	2NT	3♡*
♡ x x	3♠*	Pass
◇ x x x		
♣ x x		

Thank heavens for Transfers!

12.
East	West	East
♠ Q x x x	2NT	3◇*
♡ K J x x x	3♡*	3♠
◇ x x		
♣ x x		

Shows 5 hearts and 4 spades. Forcing to a game.

GENERAL PRINCIPLES
AND DISCUSSION POINTS

1. **THE BARON 3♣* CONVENTION,** like Stayman, is artificial, alertable and does not promise a club suit!

2. Responses to 3♣* presume 4-card suits. 2NT – 3♣* – 3NT indicates that the opener's only long suit is clubs.

3. Subsequent bids at the four level are best played as cue bids agreeing partner's suit.

4. **TRANSFER BIDS** do not promise any points and can, therefore, be used for a weak take-out at the three level but . . .

5. . . . in response to a transfer bid opener can jump directly to game holding a maximum with four trumps.

6. A 3◊* or 3♡* transfer bid followed by 3NT, although non-forcing, seeks 3-card support. Opener is requested to pick the better game accordingly.

7. A transfer followed by a new suit is natural and shape-showing (at least 5-4).

8. A transfer followed by a jump to 4NT is quantitative. Whether minimum or maximum, opener must then decide on the best strain as well as the correct level.

9. A transfer followed by a jump to 5NT asks opener to 'pick a slam' at the six level.

10. An immediate 4♣ or 4◊ response is a slam move and asks the opener to cue-bid with a suitable hand. You may prefer to use a direct response of 4♣* as Gerber. That's for you and your partner to decide.

1. *Partner opens 2NT. What would you respond?*

Hand 1a
♠ 8 7 6 5 4
♡ 2
◇ 7 6 5 4 3
♣ 3 2

0 HCP

Hand 1b
♠ J 7 5 3 2
♡ Q 6 5 3
◇ 7
♣ 9 7 5

3 HCP

Hand 1c
♠ K 9 6 5
♡ J 7 4 2
◇ 9 8 7 5
♣ 2

4 HCP

Hand 1d
♠ Q 3 2
♡ 8 6
◇ K 5 4
♣ 8 7 5 4 2

5 HCP

Hand 1e
♠ 6 5 3
♡ K Q J 6 5
◇ 4
♣ 7 6 5 4

6 HCP

Hand 1f
♠ J 2
♡ K J 7 4
◇ Q 7 5 4 2
♣ 6 5

7 HCP

2. *Partner opens 2NT. What would you respond?*

Hand 2a
♠ 6 5 4
♡ 9 7 6 4 3 2
◇ 8 4
♣ 7 2

0 HCP

Hand 2b
♠ Q 8 7 6 5 4 3
♡ 4 3
◇ 7 5
♣ 8 7

2 HCP

Hand 2c
♠ 5
♡ K J 3 2
◇ J 7 6 5 4
♣ 6 5 4

5 HCP

Hand 2d
♠ 5 4
♡ K J 3
◇ J 7 6 5 4
♣ 9 8 7

5 HCP

Hand 2e
♠ K 8 7 6
♡ Q 4 3
◇ 8 7 2
♣ J 7 3

6 HCP

Hand 2f
♠ 7
♡ K Q J 7 6 5 4
◇ J 4 3
♣ 8 2

7 HCP

Continued on next page – Answers on page 40

3. *Partner opens 2NT. What would you respond?*

Hand 3a
♠ 9 8 5 4 3 2
♡ 5 4
◇ 8 5 4
♣ 8 6

0 HCP

Hand 3b
♠ 3 2
♡ J 9 8 7 6
◇ 4
♣ 9 7 5 3 2

1 HCP

Hand 3c
♠ 9 7 5
♡ K 9 6 4 3 2
◇ 5 4
♣ 3 2

3 HCP

Hand 3d
♠ A Q 3 2
♡ Q 7 6 5
◇ 8 7 6 5
♣ 6

8 HCP

Hand 3e
♠ Q J 7 5 3
♡ J 7 6 5
◇ 5
♣ A Q 2

10 HCP

Hand 3f
♠ K Q 8 6
♡ A 3 2
◇ K 7 6
♣ K 6 5

15 HCP

4. *And a few more for luck!*

Hand 4a
♠ K J 5
♡ Q 7 5
◇ 3 2
♣ Q 9 8 7 5

8 HCP

Hand 4b
♠ K J 7 5
♡ K 9 8 7 6
◇ Q 3 2
♣ 9

9 HCP

Hand 4c
♠ Q 8 6
♡ K J 8 7 5 2
◇ K 6
♣ J 2

10 HCP

Hand 4d
♠ A 2
♡ 6 5 4
◇ K Q J 7 6 5
♣ J 6

11 HCP

Hand 4e
♠ K 9 8
♡ A 5 4 3
◇ J 7 4
♣ K J 7

12 HCP

Hand 4f
♠ A Q 7
♡ K Q J
◇ 5 4 3
♣ J 8 7 6

13 HCP

Answers on page 40

1a	1b	1c
3♡*	3♠*	3♣*

1d	1e	1f
3NT	3◊*	3♣*

2a	2b	2c
3◊*	3♡*	3♣*

2d	2e	2f
3NT	3NT	4♡

3a	3b	3c
3♡*	3◊*	3◊*

3d	3e	3f
3♣*	3♠*	5NT

4a	4b	4c
3NT	3◊*	4♡

4d	4e	4f
4◊	4NT	6NT

CHAPTER THREE

TRANSFERS OVER 1NT

Attributed to Oswald Jacoby, Transfer responses to a 1NT opening bid are one of the most important advances made in the theory of bidding in recent years. An amazing invention, indeed! How did we ever cope before? "Not very well at all!" would be my answer.

As the weak 1NT opener crops up so frequently, it is really important to play a system that is effective. All experts play Transfers, so that should be recommendation enough. Unfortunately there are many variations of the Transfer system on the market that are all equally playable, effective, different – and imperfect! With each version kitted out with minor defects and flaws, how will you know which treatment is best for you? For the moment you will have to make do with reading about my personal favourite teaching method, but it would be wise to shop around once you feel confident enough to choose your own.

Fortunately Stayman, as you know it, still exists but your present interpretation may suffer from a small knock-on effect as you integrate it with your preferred Transfer system. This will be a small price to pay for superior results, honest!

You will be forgiven for thinking that perhaps there is nothing wrong with the good old-fashioned methods you are already playing but – and it is a big 'but' – without the aid of Transfers scope for developing the auction is definitely limited. We all know how important it is to get to the best contract and the invention of Transfers has unquestionably increased the odds in our favour of achieving that aim. You really can't be a budding expert without them, so do have a go!

The basic theory is that after partner has opened 1NT (regardless of the strength) an initial response at the two level is no longer natural. 2♣ is still retained as Stayman but 2◊, 2♡, 2♠ and 2NT are all artificial and alertable relay bids. Each conveys a specific meaning together with a command to partner. In all Transfer systems, 2◊ shows at least 5 hearts and 2♡ shows at least 5 spades.

Time to take a look at the full system. It may not be the simplest, it may not be the best, but it does incorporate all the advantages of Transfers without being too complex. I'm sure you can't wait any longer, so . . .

TRANSFERS OVER 1NT
CONVENTION

The standard Transfer systems all have three bids in common . . .

2♣*	Stayman – asking for 4 card majors.
2◇ *	A relay showing 5+ hearts
2♡*	A relay showing 5+ spades

. . . and none of these bids promise any points!

1NT – 2◇* 2♡* – **Pass**	0-10 HCP. 5+ hearts.
1NT – 2◇* 2♡* – **2♠**	11-12 HCP with 5 hearts and 4 spades. It is invitational and can be passed.
1NT – 2◇* 2♡* – **2NT**	11-12 HCP. Presumed to be balanced with a 5-card heart suit. However, you also need to accommodate 5-4-3-1 and 5-4-2-2 shapes. It is *not forcing* and invites game in no-trumps or hearts with a maximum.
1NT – 2◇* 2♡* – **3♣/◇**	13+ HCP with 5+ hearts and 4+ cards in the bid minor. It is game-forcing.
1NT – 2◇* 2♡* – **3♡**	10-12 HCP with a 6-card suit. Invites game in hearts or no-trumps.

TRANSFERS OVER 1NT
CONVENTION CONTINUED

1NT – 2◇* 2♡* – 3NT	13-18 HCP with 5 hearts and a balanced hand, i.e. 5-3-3-2. Opener is asked to pick the right game.
1NT – 2♡* 2♠* – Pass	0-10 HCP. 5+ spades.
1NT – 2♡* 2♠* – 2NT	11-12 HCP. Presumed to be balanced with a 5-card spade suit. However, you also need to accommodate 5-4-3-1 and 5-4-2-2 distributions. It is *not forcing* and invites game in no-trumps or spades with a maximum.
1NT – 2♡* 2♠* – 3♣/◇	13+ HCP with 5 spades and 4+ cards in the bid minor. It is game-forcing.
1NT – 2♡* 2♠* – 3♡	11-12 HCP with 5 spades and 4 hearts. It is invitational and can be passed.
1NT – 2♡* 2♠* – 3♠	10-12 HCP with a 6-card suit. Invites game in spades or no-trumps.
1NT – 2♡* 2♠* – 4♡	Game values and 5-5 in the majors.
1NT – 2♡* 2♠* – 3NT	13-18 HCP with 5 spades and a balanced hand, i.e. 5-3-3-2. Opener is asked to pick the right game.
1NT – 2♠*	Asks if opener is minimum or maximum. *(See note 8 on page 48 for a full account.)*
1NT – 2NT*	An artificial relay ('puppet') requesting opener to bid 3♣. *(See note 9 on page 49 for a full account.)*

TRANSFERS OVER 1NT
CONVENTION CONTINUED

1NT – 3♣/♢/♡/♠   13+ HCP. Natural and forcing to game with
                      at least a 6-card suit and likely slam interest.
                      Cue-bidding is expected with a suitable
                      hand.

1NT – 3NT   13-18 HCP. All game bids are to play.
                      Natural. May contain a 6-card minor *(see
                      Note 7 on page 48)*.

1NT – 4♣*   With a 3♣ bid available for a natural call,
                      you might as well play this as Gerber!

1NT – 4♡/♠   Sometimes partner doesn't play the cards as
                      well as you! Joking apart, the contract may
                      be a better prospect played from your side.
                      Make sure you have at least a 6-card suit
                      and game values.

1NT – 4NT   19-20 HCP. *Quantitative.*
                      4-3-3-3 precisely (any order).

The whole system may seem a little awesome at first glance; while
you catch your breath, I'll explain the benefits of Transfers to you.
(Compare with Chapter 2.)

BENEFITS OF TRANSFERS

1. Transfer bids enable the majority of (but by no means all) contracts to be played by the 1NT opener. If the strong hand is concealed, vulnerable tenaces will be protected from the opening lead and this will also serve to make the subsequent defence more difficult. If the dummy is going to be as weak as in the example below, you can see the merits of this aspect:

West	East
♠ A 10 3	♠ J 9 8 7 4
♡ K 6 5 4	♡ 7 3
◇ A 4 3	◇ Q J 6 5
♣ K 6 2	♣ 5 4

West	East
1NT	2♡*
2♠*	Pass

Any lead will be helpful if West is declarer here. Played by East, however, the two kings will be exposed to an immediate attack by the defenders.

2. Transfer bids can provide ideal solutions to awkward problems. Here are a couple of good examples:

a)

West	East
♠ K J 6	♠ 4 3
♡ J 6	♡ Q 9 8 7 2
◇ A Q 2	◇ J 6 3
♣ Q 7 6 5 4	♣ A K J

West	East
1NT	2◇*
2♡*	2NT
Pass	

The ability to show a balanced raise to 2NT with a 5-card major is just magic and impossible if you don't play Transfers.

b)

West	East
♠ Q 3	♠ A K J 7 6 5
♡ K 8 7 6	♡ Q J
◇ A K 3 2	◇ 5 4
♣ 5 4 3	♣ 9 8 7

West	East
1NT	2♡*
2♠*	3♠
Pass	

Responder's assets here would be equally impossible to describe without the aid of a Transfer system. Now you can invite game with a 6-card major. Don't go away – it gets even better!

3. Transfer bids add a new dimension to the bidding after 1NT, leaving more room to explore for the best contract at the lowest possible level. Fancy being able to tell partner you have two suits and still be below game at the three level!

West	East
♠ 5 4	♠ A K J 7 2
♡ K Q J 10	♡ 6 5 2
◇ A K 7 2	◇ Q
♣ 7 6 5	♣ Q J 9 8

West	East
1NT	2♡*
2♠*	3♣
3NT	

How many Easts would have felt comfortable about a resting spot of 3NT here? Well, once you have announced nine black cards, you can leave partner to make the final decision.

BENEFITS OF TRANSFERS CONTINUED

4. Last but not least, the 1NT bidder can contribute to the auction by 'breaking' the Transfer command holding four or more of partner's suit. Keeping your opponents out of a making contract will be one of your rewards even if it does entail chalking up a minus score:

a)
West	East
♠ 4 3	♠ 8 7
♡ J 7 6 5	♡ K Q 8 4 3 2
◊ A K 8 7	◊ J 5
♣ A 3 2	♣ 8 7 6

West	East
1NT	2◊*
3♡*	Pass

Allowing the opponents to protect at the two level is a generous gesture. With a sure-fire part-score in spades available and possibly a game contract their way, a small sacrifice in hearts could be a very good investment in an attempt to keep them out.

Your pre-emptive manoeuvre can also work constructively when there's a borderline decision concerning game prospects for your side:

b)
West	East
♠ A 9 3 2	♠ K 8 7 6 5 4
♡ J 7 6	♡ 4
◊ Q J 6	◊ K 5 4
♣ A 3 2	♣ K 5 4

West	East
1NT	2♡*
3♠*	4♠

Facing four-card spade support any bridge player would want to chance their luck in game. A transfer break by West fulfils that dream!

GENERAL PRINCIPLES
AND DISCUSSION POINTS

1. A relay bid says *nothing* about the suit actually bid!

2. The 2◊* and 2♡* relay bids can be made with *no points*!

3. The only artificial bids you have to remember are all played at the two level and one of those is Stayman 2♣.

4. After the initial transfer bid all other bids are natural.

5. As with Stayman, Transfers do not apply after direct intervention.

6. The only bid which is 'lost' playing Transfers is a weakness take-out into 2◊ – but this will be a minor disappointment! (Excuse the pun!)

7. To express an invitational hand with a 6-card minor, shoot 3NT and hope for the best!

8. The **BARON 2♠** element needs further clarification;
    The 2♠* response is used holding one of the following two types of balanced hands (**BA**ron,**BA**lanced!):

    a) 11 HCP or 12 HCP – and a balanced invitational raise to 3NT with *no* major suit interest.

    b) 18+ HCP. Balanced with slam interest. May have a 4-card major. *Not* 4-3-3-3 but possibly 4-4-4-1 and 17+ HCP.

    In response to the 2♠* enquiry:
    2NT* shows a minimum 1NT opener
    3♣* shows a maximum 1NT opener
    (N.B. The 3♣* response does *not* show clubs!)

    After a 2NT* or 3♣* response all bids at the three level show four card suits and indicate slam interest with 18+ HCP (17+ if 4-4-4-1 type).

GENERAL PRINCIPLES
AND DISCUSSION POINTS CONTINUED

9. **THE 2NT RESPONSE** needs further clarification too:
Opener *must* bid 3♣* without exception. Hands which can now be described fall into two categories.

   a) A weak hand with a 6+ card minor.
   In response to 3♣*:
   Pass shows clubs.
   3◇ shows diamonds.

   b) A game-going hand with at least 5-5 in the minors.
   In response to 3♣*:
   3♡* or 3♠* shows a singleton or void in the bid suit and also indicates slam interest. Opener should now make an intelligent bid!
   3NT shows no slam interest and requests opener to pick a game, i.e. 3NT or 5♣/5◇.

10. If you hold one or both major-suits in response to a 1NT opening bid, here is a resumé of when you should Transfer and when you should use Stayman.

(A) STAYMAN

1. Weak hands with at least 5-4 in the majors, 0-10 HCP.
   (With these hands, sign off at the two level in the best fit.)
2. One or two 4-card majors, 11-17 HCP.
   (Promises at least game-invitational values)
3. Game-forcing hands with 5-4 in the majors.
   (If partner responds 2◇*, you jump to three of your 5-card major for partner to tell you if he has 3-card support.)

   e.g.   1NT – 2♣*
           2◇* – 3♡ **or 3♠**   game-forcing with a 5-card suit.

   *N.B. Hands with slam interest opposite a major-suit fit and a maximum opening bid should **not** be described by using Stayman. If you proceed via the Baron 2♠ response with these hand types, you can ensure reaching a 6NT contract when there is no fit. (See Note 8b, page 48).*

GENERAL PRINCIPLES
AND DISCUSSION POINTS CONTINUED

(B) TRANSFERS

1. Weak hands with one major of at least five cards. 0-10 HCP. (To play at the two level.)
2. Invitational or game-going hands with one major suit of at least 5 cards, 11+ HCP.
3. Invitational hands with 5-4 or 5-5 in the majors, 11-12 HCP.

e.g.	1NT – 2♡*	
	2♠* – 3♡	5-4 or 5-5
	1NT – 2◇*	
	2♡* – 2♠	4-5

11. Last but not least, if you have opened 1NT and partner transfers into a major in which you hold four cards – jump to three of that suit. You may be disobeying partner's 'command' but it gets good results most of the time! *(See Note 4, page 47.)*

1. | East | West | East |
    |------|------|------|
    | ♠ x x | 1NT | 2◇* |
    | ♡ Q x x x x | 2♡* | Pass |
    | ◇ x x x | | |
    | ♣ x x x | | |

    A weak take-out with 5+ hearts.

2. | East | West | East |
    |------|------|------|
    | ♠ A x x x | 1NT | 2◇* |
    | ♡ K J x x x | 2♡* | 2♠ |
    | ◇ K x | | |
    | ♣ x x | | |

    Invitational with 5 hearts and 4 spades.

3. | East | West | East |
    |------|------|------|
    | ♠ A x | 1NT | 2◇* |
    | ♡ Q J x x x | 2♡* | 2NT |
    | ◇ J x x | | |
    | ♣ K x | | |

    Invitational with 5 hearts. Usually balanced but may be semi-balanced or even unbalanced.

4. | East | West | East |
    |------|------|------|
    | ♠ x x | 1NT | 2◇* |
    | ♡ A K x x x | 2♡* | 3◇ |
    | ◇ K J x x | | |
    | ♣ K x | | |

    At least 5 hearts and 4 diamonds. Game-forcing.

5. | East | West | East |
    |------|------|------|
    | ♠ J x x | 1NT | 2◇* |
    | ♡ K Q J x x x | 2♡* | 3♡ |
    | ◇ A x | | |
    | ♣ x x | | |

    Invitational with a 6-card suit.

6.

East	West	East
♠ A Q x	1NT	2◇*
♡ A J x x x	2♡*	3NT
◇ x x		
♣ K x x		

A balanced raise to game with 5 hearts.

7.

East	West	East
♠ J x x x x x	1NT	2♡*
♡ x x	2♠*	Pass
◇ x x		
♣ x x x		

A weak take-out with 5+ spades.

8.

East	West	East
♠ K Q x x x	1NT	2♡*
♡ Q x	2♠*	2NT
◇ J x x		
♣ K x x		

Invitational with 5 spades and may be unbalanced!

9.

East	West	East
♠ A Q x x x	1NT	2♡*
♡ x	2♠*	3♣
◇ A x x		
♣ A J x x		

At least 5 spades and 4 clubs. Game-forcing.

10.

East	West	East
♠ A K x x x	1NT	2♡*
♡ Q J x x	2♠*	3♡
◇ J x		
♣ x x		

Invitational with 5 spades and 4 hearts.

11.

East	West	East
♠ A K J x x x	1NT	2♡*
♡ x x	2♠*	3♠
◊ J x x		
♣ Q x		

Invitational with a 6-card suit.

12.

East	West	East
♠ K J x x	1NT	2♡*
♡ K J x x	2♠*	4♡
◊ A J		
♣ x		

At least 5-5 in the majors. Opener to give preference.

13.

East	West	East
♠ A K Q x x	1NT	2♡*
♡ x x	2♠*	3NT
◊ K x x		
♣ Q x x		

A balanced raise to game with 5 spades.

14.

East	West	East
♠ K J x	1NT	2♠*
♡ Q x x x		
◊ A x x		
♣ J x x		

A quantitative raise. 11-12 HCP. N.B. No shortage, no Stayman!

15.

East	West	East
♠ Q x x	1NT	2♠*
♡ Q x		
◊ A K x x		
♣ A K J x		

A quantitative raise with 18+ HCP (17+ HCP if 4-4-4-1).

16.

East	West	East
♠ x x	1NT	2NT*
♡ J x	3♣*	Pass
◇ K x		
♣ Q J x x x x		

A 'puppet' to 3♣.

17.

East	West	East
♠ x x	1NT	2NT*
♡ J x x	3♣*	3◇
◇ K J x x x		
♣ Q x		

A 'puppet' to 3♣ converted to diamonds.

18.

East	West	East
♠ J	1NT	2NT*
♡ A x	3♣*	3NT
◇ K J x x		
♣ K J x x		

5-5 in the minors. No slam interest. Opener to choose between 3NT, 5♣, or 5◇. *(See Note 9b, page 49.)*

19.

East	West	East
♠ x x	1NT	2NT*
♡ x	3♣*	3♡*
◇ A K Q x x		
♣ K Q J x x		

5-5 in the minors with slam interest and a heart 'Splinter'.

LEARNING BY EXAMPLES

1. *Partner opens 1NT. What would you respond?*

Hand 1a
♠ 5 4
♡ 9 8 7 6 5
◊ 7 6 5 4
♣ 3 2

0 HCP

Hand 1b
♠ K 7 6 4 2
♡ 4 3
◊ 9 7 3
♣ 5 3 2

3 HCP

Hand 1c
♠ 9 7
♡ Q 6 4
◊ J 7 6 5 4
♣ J 8 7

4 HCP

Hand 1d
♠ 8 7 2
♡ 7 6 5
◊ Q 3
♣ K 8 7 6 5

5 HCP

Hand 1e
♠ 4 3
♡ 9 7 4
◊ 6 5
♣ K Q J 8 7 6

6 HCP

Hand 1f
♠ A 7 4
♡ 2
◊ Q J 9 8 5 4
♣ 8 7 5

7 HCP

2. *Partner opens 1NT. What would you respond?*

Hand 2a
♠ Q 7 6 5 4
♡ J 5 4 3
◊ 3
♣ A J 6

8 HCP

Hand 2b
♠ J 6 5 4 3
♡ Q 9 7 5 3
◊ K Q
♣ J

9 HCP

Hand 2c
♠ K 8 6 3
♡ Q J 6 5
◊ A 3 2
♣ 7 6

10 HCP

Hand 2d
♠ K Q 8 7 5 3
♡ A 5 3
◊ J 8
♣ 5 4

10 HCP

Hand 2e
♠ K 4
♡ K J 9 8 6 5
◊ 8 3 2
♣ K 7

10 HCP

Hand 2f
♠ A J 7 6 5
♡ K J 6 5
◊ 7 6
♣ Q 2

11 HCP

Continued on next page – Answers on page 58

3. *Partner opens 1NT. What would you respond?*

Hand 3a	Hand 3b	Hand 3c
♠ A 7 6	♠ 8 7 6	♠ A J 7 4
♡ K Q J 7 6	♡ K Q 2	♡ J 8 6 4 2
◊ J 3 2	◊ A J 9 8 7	◊ K 6 4
♣ 8 7	♣ J 6	♣ Q
11 HCP	11 HCP	11 HCP

Hand 3d	Hand 3e	Hand 3f
♠ Q J 7 6	♠ A 4 2	♠ K Q 6 5
♡ J 6 5	♡ 7 6	♡ A 9 8 7 6
◊ K 9 7	◊ Q 2	◊ K J 4
♣ A J 3	♣ A Q 8 6 5 4	♣ 2
12 HCP	12 HCP	13 HCP

4. *Partner opens 1NT. What would you respond?*

Hand 4a	Hand 4b	Hand 4c
♠ A K 8 6 5	♠ A J 9 8	♠ 4
♡ J 7	♡ K J 6	♡ Q 5
◊ A J 6 2	◊ 4 3 2	◊ A J 8 6 3
♣ 5 4	♣ A 7 5	♣ K Q J 7 6
13 HCP	13 HCP	13 HCP

Hand 4d	Hand 4e	Hand 4f
♠ A 5 4	♠ A 9 8 7 6	♠ 7 2
♡ K J 8 7 6	♡ A Q J 6 5	♡ A K 9 3 2
◊ 2	◊ 8 6	◊ 2
♣ A Q 5 4	♣ K	♣ A K 8 7 6
14 HCP	14 HCP	14 HCP

Continued on next page – Answers on page 58

5. *Partner opens 1NT. What would you respond?*

Hand 5a	Hand 5b	Hand 5c
♠ —	♠ J 7	♠ A K J 9 6 5
♡ 3	♡ A 2	♡ 6
◊ A K J 7 6 5	◊ K Q J 7 6 5	◊ A 8 4
♣ A Q 9 8 7 6	♣ K 3 2	♣ K 6 5
14 HCP	14 HCP	15 HCP

Hand 5d	Hand 5e	Hand 5f
♠ K Q J 5	♠ K Q 3	♠ A 6 5
♡ A J 6	♡ A Q J 7 6 5	♡ K 9 8 7 6
◊ 6 5	◊ A J 6	◊ —
♣ A J 7 3	♣ 2	♣ A K Q J 6
16 HCP	17 HCP	17 HCP

6. *Partner opens 1NT. What would you respond?*

Hand 6a	Hand 6b	Hand 6c
♠ K Q 5	♠ K Q 5 4	♠ 5 4
♡ A J 7 2	♡ A J 7 2	♡ A 2
◊ K J 6	◊ K J 6	◊ K Q J 8 7 6
♣ K 6 2	♣ K 6	♣ A K 6
17 HCP	17 HCP	17 HCP

Hand 6d	Hand 6e	Hand 6f
♠ 2	♠ A K Q J	♠ Q J 5
♡ K Q 8 7	♡ 4	♡ A J 6
◊ A K J 6	◊ A K Q J 6 5 4	◊ K Q J
♣ A Q 4 3	♣ 3	♣ A Q 3 2
19 HCP	20 HCP	20 HCP

Answers on page 58

1a	**1b**	**1c**
2◊*	2♡*	Pass
1d	**1e**	**1f**
Pass	2NT*	2NT*
2a	**2b**	**2c**
2♣*	2♣*	Pass
2d	**2e**	**2f**
2♡*	2◊*	2♡*
3a	**3b**	**3c**
2◊*	2♠*	2◊*
3d	**3e**	**3f**
2♠*	3NT	2♣*
4a	**4b**	**4c**
2♡*	3NT	2NT*
4d	**4e**	**4f**
2◊*	2♡*	2◊*
5a	**5b**	**5c**
2NT*	3NT	3♠
5d	**5e**	**5f**
2♣*	3♡	2◊*
6a	**6b**	**6c**
3NT	2♣*	3◊
6d	**6e**	**6f**
2♠*	4♣*	4NT

Practise your rebid on the examples where partner:

  a) Completes the Transfer or Puppet.

  b) 'Breaks' the Transfer to three of the major.

  c) Responds 2◊ to any Stayman enquiry.

See Chapter 14 for Defence to Transfers.

CHAPTER FOUR

LANDY 2♣ DEFENCE TO 1NT

If you want to compete over a 1NT opening bid, the Landy 2♣ convention, devised by Alvin Landy, gets my vote. It's simple, it's effective, and it has been my favourite ever since I can remember.

This particular convention concentrates on locating a major-suit fit and, as such, might be labelled as being somewhat limited. Sure enough you will meet players who prefer more complex methods and, as usual, the choice is yours. At the end of the day, you can wade through a host of conventions but for your first step into the arena I believe this is your best option.

Unlike Stayman, which asks you if you hold a 4-card major, Landy *shows both*. Legally it can be used with just four cards in each major but this treatment can prove hazardous even for us experienced mortals! Take my advice and guarantee your partner a minimum of nine cards between hearts and spades, and you will live to tell the tale!

LANDY 2♣ DEFENCE TO 1NT CONVENTION

A 2♣* OVERCALL SHOWS

1. The values to compete at the two level (usually 10-15 HCP).
2. At least 5-4 in the majors.

It is artificial and alertable.

RESPONSES

2◇*
: A forcing relay. May be weak or strong. *This bid is also artificial and alertable.* **It does not promise any points!** Your hand will contain either:

    a) Equal length in both majors. 0+ HCP. (Intending to pass the response if 0-9 HCP)

    b) At least one 3-card major with 10+ HCP. (i.e. at least invitational values)

    c) A game-force with a 6+ card minor suit. (Bid 2◇* then 3♣ or 3◇)

    The Landy bidder replies showing his longer major or bids 2♡ with equal length.

2♡/2♠
: Longer major. 0-9 HCP. (Usually 3 cards)

2NT
: Natural and invitational. 10-12 HCP. (No major-suit interest)

3♣/3◇
: Natural and invitational. 10-12 HCP. (No major-suit interest)

3♡/3♠
: Limit raise with four trumps. 10-12 HCP.

LANDY 2♣ DEFENCE TO 1NT
CONVENTION CONTINUED

Game bids   To play. Oh! and I nearly forgot . . .

. . . Pass!   At your peril! Only a good idea if you have a weak hand with a load of clubs.

IF 2♣* IS DOUBLED the responses are slightly different!

Pass   Clubs. 5+ cards.

2◇   Diamonds. 5+ cards.

Redouble   Asks partner to bid his longer major (hearts with equal length).

2♡/2♠   Major-suit preference.

3♡/3♠   Pre-emptive with at least four trumps.

GENERAL PRINCIPLES
AND DISCUSSION POINTS

1. The strength of your opponent's 1NT opening bid is completely irrelevant. Your overcall will be just as effective over a mini, a weak, or a strong no-trump.

2. It can be used in both the direct overcalling seat and the protective seat, and whether or not you are a passed hand.

3. To overcall 2♣* partner is going to expect you to hold the equivalent values for an opening bid. Depending on your distribution this could be quite wide-ranging and even include some strong hands that are not suitable to make a penalty double of 1NT.

4. The 2♣* bid is not forcing – so beware!

5. You cannot use the 2♣* bid to show a single-suited hand with clubs. If you have one of these you must make a jump overcall of 3♣.

6. All other suit overcalls are natural.

7. If you are 6-4 in the majors it is preferable to overcall your 6-card suit.

8. By agreement, an overcall of 2NT shows a game-forcing two-suited hand (at least 5-5).

9. If you think that this chapter is difficult, don't bother looking at any other conventions in defence to 1NT!

1. *Your right-hand opponent opens 1NT. What do you overcall?*

Hand 1a	**Hand 1b**	**Hand 1c**
♠ A J 6 5 4	♠ K Q J 3 2	♠ J 8 7 6 5
♡ A J 5 4 3	♡ J 6 5 4	♡ A K Q J 2
◇ 3 2	◇ K J 4	◇ 4
♣ 3	♣ 2	♣ J 6
10 HCP	11 HCP	12 HCP

Hand 1d	**Hand 1e**	**Hand 1f**
♠ 5 4	♠ Q J 7 6	♠ A 5
♡ 9 2	♡ K 7 6 3	♡ Q 5
◇ K Q 9 6 5 4	◇ Q 9 6	◇ K 2
♣ A K 5	♣ K Q	♣ K J 9 8 7 6 5
12 HCP	13 HCP	13 HCP

2. *Your right-hand opponent opens 1NT. What do you overcall?*

Hand 2a	**Hand 2b**	**Hand 2c**
♠ K Q 8 7 2	♠ K J 8 7 6 5	♠ J 8
♡ A 7 5 3	♡ A Q 6 4	♡ A Q 3
◇ A 4 3 2	◇ K 2	◇ Q 3
♣ —	♣ 3	♣ K J 8 6 5 3
13 HCP	13 HCP	13 HCP

Hand 2d	**Hand 2e**	**Hand 2f**
♠ K 9 8 3	♠ A 5 4 3	♠ A 5 4 3
♡ K J 9 7 4	♡ K Q 9 6 5 4	♡ A K Q J 4 3
◇ A 5	◇ K	◇ 2
♣ K 4	♣ Q J	♣ J 2
14 HCP	15 HCP	15 HCP

Continued on next page – Answers on page 66

3. *Make your response to partner's Landy 2♣ overcall:*
   (1NT) – 2♣* – (Pass) – ?

Hand 3a	**Hand 3b**	**Hand 3c**
♠ 4 3 2	♠ 8 7 6	♠ J 7 2
♡ 4 3 2	♡ 5 3	♡ J 7 6
◊ 4 3 2	◊ 8 7 6 5	◊ 3
♣ 5 4 3 2	♣ 8 7 6 5	♣ 9 7 5 4 3 2
0 HCP	0 HCP	2 HCP

Hand 3d	**Hand 3e**	**Hand 3f**
♠ K 2	♠ Q 5	♠ 4
♡ J 4 2	♡ Q 5	♡ 5 4
◊ 8 7 6 5 4	◊ 9 8 4 3	◊ 8 3 2
♣ 4 3 2	♣ J 7 6 5 4	♣ K Q J 9 8 7 6
4 HCP	5 HCP	6 HCP

4. *Make your response to partner's Landy 2♣ overcall:*
   (1NT) – 2♣* – (Pass) – ?

Hand 4a	**Hand 4b**	**Hand 4c**
♠ 9 7 5 3	♠ A 7 5 2	♠ J 7
♡ K Q J	♡ J 6 4 3	♡ Q 7 3
◊ J 6 5 4	◊ 7 6	◊ A 8 7 6 5 4
♣ 3 2	♣ K J 6	♣ Q 2
7 HCP	9 HCP	9 HCP

Hand 4d	**Hand 4e**	**Hand 4f**
♠ K Q 6	♠ Q 4	♠ K J 5 4
♡ 8 6 3	♡ J 7	♡ 5
◊ K 8 6 4	◊ K J 9 8	◊ A 6 5 4
♣ Q 3 2	♣ Q J 8 7 6	♣ Q 4 3 2
10 HCP	10 HCP	10 HCP

Continued on next page – Answers on page 66

Landy 2♣ Defence to 1NT

5. *Make your response to partner's Landy 2♣ overcall:*
   (1NT) – 2♣* – (Pass) – ?

Hand 5a	**Hand 5b**	**Hand 5c**
♠ 5 3	♠ A J 6	♠ 8 6 2
♡ 8 7	♡ Q 6	♡ Q J 7 6
◇ Q 4 3	◇ K 5 4	◇ Q 2
♣ A K J 8 7 6	♣ J 7 5 4 2	♣ A Q J 7
10 HCP	11 HCP	12 HCP

Hand 5d	**Hand 5e**	**Hand 5f**
♠ 2	♠ K Q 8	♠ J 2
♡ 3 2	♡ 6 5 4	♡ A K 7 3
◇ A Q J 7 2	◇ A 4 3	◇ K Q J 6
♣ K Q J 9 8	♣ A J 8 7	♣ J 6 3
13 HCP	14 HCP	15 HCP

Answers on page 66

1a	1b	1c
2♣*	2♣*	2♣*

1d	1e	1f
2◇	Pass	3♣

2a	2b	2c
2♣*	2♠	Pass

2d	2e	2f
2♣*	2♡	Dbl

3a	3b	3c
2◇*	2♠	2◇*

3d	3e	3f
2♡	2◇*	Pass

4a	4b	4c
2♠	2◇*	2♡

4d	4e	4f
2◇*	2NT	3♠

5a	5b	5c
3♣	2◇*	3♡

5d	5e	5f
3NT	2◇*	4♡

CHAPTER FIVE

NEGATIVE DOUBLES

Partner opens 1◊. Your right-hand opponent overcalls 1♠ and you look forlornly at your options holding:

♠ 5 4 3
♡ K Q J 3
◊ 3 2
♣ 6 5 4 3

You only have six high-card points but it would have been enough to reply 1♡ without the intervention. How about 1NT? While stoppers are not generally necessary for suggesting a no-trump contract, there is a sensible proviso to have one in a suit bid by your opponents. So much for that idea, then! As you do not have the requirements for a response at the two level, it looks like you will have to Pass, hoping for a chance to describe your assets later. Not so fast! There is a way – but you and your partner will need to be on the same wavelength – as the enigmatic Double comes to your rescue.

Call it the Negative double, the Informatory double or the Sputnik double – it matters not – as they are all essentially a variation of the take-out double with which you are already familiar. So, how can a double in a position that has previously been intended to be for penalties now be used to carry a 'take-out' message without causing confusion?

Like many conventions that you want to adopt, new meanings of bids must replace old ones and as long as you are not losing a valuable, natural bid in the process there's really nothing to worry about – other than partner forgetting the system! You will still be able to take a penalty when it's appropriate, but that option will have to be via a different route. Let this be a warning to all you frivolous overcallers who think they can escape the axe when their opponents are playing Negative Doubles! In fact, punishing the enemy just couldn't be easier! How? Well, you'll have to wait and see!

NEGATIVE DOUBLES CONVENTION

A "Negative Double" replaces the standard penalty double by responder after partner has opened the bidding with one of a suit and your right-hand opponent overcalls in another suit.

'Double' promises four cards in the unbid major or majors. If both majors have been bid the double guarantees four cards in each of the minor suits.

After an overcall at the one level a 'double' shows 6+ HCP.
After an overcall at the two level a 'double' shows 8+ HCP.
After an overcall at the three level a 'double' shows 10+ HCP.

These doubles are all alertable!

Examples

1◇ – (1♠) – **Dbl*** Take-out with 4 hearts. 6+ HCP.

1♣ – (1♡) – **Dbl*** Take-out with 4 spades. 6+ HCP.
        (**N.B.** A bid of 1♠ promises 5+ spades)

1♣ – (1◇) – **Dbl*** Take-out with 4-4 in both majors. 6+ HCP.

1♡ – (1♠) – **Dbl*** Take-out with 4-4 in both minors. 6+ HCP.

1♡ – (2♣) – **Dbl*** Take-out with 4 spades. 8+ points.

1♠ – (3♣) – **Dbl*** Take-out with 4 hearts. 10+ points.

GENERAL PRINCIPLES AND DISCUSSION POINTS

1. The double is used primarily to describe hands that have become awkward to bid because of the overcall.

e.g.

East	East
♠ x x x	♠ A x x x
♡ A K x x	♡ K x x x
◊ J x x	◊ x x
♣ x x x	♣ Q x x

West	North	East	South		West	North	East	South
1♣	1♠	?			1◊	2♣	?	

If you double here, it will show four cards in the unbid major or majors. Perfect!

2. Although there is no limit as to how high you can play a negative double, most people play them up to an overcall of 3♠ or 4◊. Whichever level you do decide on, remember to let partner in on the secret!

e.g.

East	East
♠ x x	♠ A J x x
♡ A K x x	♡ x x x
◊ K Q J x	◊ K J x
♣ x x x	♣ Q x x

West	North	East	South		West	North	East	South
1♠	3♣	?			1◊	2♡	?	

A double on either of these hands tells partner you have the unbid major.

GENERAL PRINCIPLES
AND DISCUSSION POINTS CONTINUED

3. If one major has been bid, a double promises four cards in the other one but it does not guarantee the unbid minor. Neither does it deny support for partner's minor!

e.g.

East	East
♠ Q x x x	♠ x x x
♡ x x	♡ K J x x
◊ K Q J x	◊ A x
♣ x x x	♣ Q x x x

West	North	East	South
1◊	1♡	Dbl*	

West	North	East	South
1♠	2♣	Dbl*	

4. Responding 1♠ after an overcall of 1♡ shows at least a 5-card suit. This is a particularly useful understanding to have for those irritating occasions when your left-hand opponent preempts the auction in hearts.

e.g.

East	East
♠ K x x x x	♠ J x x x
♡ K x	♡ x x x
◊ x x x	◊ K J x x
♣ x x x	♣ J x

West	North	East	South	
1♣	1♡	1♠		*but*

West	North	East	South
1♣	1♡	Dbl*	

GENERAL PRINCIPLES
AND DISCUSSION POINTS CONTINUED

5. You can also use the negative double after an overcall of 1♠ when you have more than four hearts, but are not strong enough for a change of suit at the two level.

e.g.

East	East
♠ x x x	♠ J x
♡ J x x x x	♡ Q x x x x
◊ A Q x	◊ A Q x
♣ x x	♣ x x x

West	North	East	South		West	North	East	South
1♣	1♠	Dbl*		*but*	1◊	1♠	2♡	

After an initial double on the first example you might get a chance to bid your hearts later. That will convey that you have 5+ hearts and less than 9 HCP.

Give yourself a 6- or 7-card suit and fewer than 9 HCP, and it would be even more appropriate to bid some number of hearts on the next round of the auction after your initial double.

e.g.

East	East
♠ J x	♠ x x
♡ K x x x x x	♡ A x x x x x x
◊ K J x	◊ x
♣ x x	♣ Q x x

West	North	East	South		West	North	East	South
1♣	1♠	Dbl*	Pass	*or*	1◊	1♠	Dbl*	Pass
2♣	Pass	2♡			2◊	Pass	2♡	

As a general rule, therefore, an immediate change of suit by you is forcing after your right-hand opponent has overcalled. *Ergo*, a change of suit will *not* be forcing if your first call was a negative double.

GENERAL PRINCIPLES
AND DISCUSSION POINTS CONTINUED

6. In response to the negative double opener should continue the bidding as if his partner had replied naturally in the suit that is promised by the double.

e.g.

	West					West		
	♠ K x x					♠ x x		
	♡ Q x					♡ A J x x		
	◇ A J x x x x					◇ K x		
	♣ K x					♣ A K J x x		

West	North	East	South		West	North	East	South
1◇	1♠	Dbl*	Pass		1♣	1♠	Dbl*	Pass
2◇					3♡			

7. Passing the negative double is not out of the question either! Perhaps the opener has a very good trump holding and wishes to convert the 'take-out' double into penalties.

e.g.

	West					West		
	♠ x x					♠ A J x x		
	♡ A K x x x					♡ A K J x		
	◇ K Q J x					◇ x		
	♣ J x					♣ J x x		

West	North	East	South		West	North	East	South
1♡	2◇	Dbl*	Pass		1♠	2♡	Dbl*	Pass
Pass!					Pass!			

GENERAL PRINCIPLES
AND DISCUSSION POINTS CONTINUED

8. If you want to penalise the overcaller, you have to pass and await partner's re-opening double. Hopefully you won't have to wait too long! You will then be able to convert this take-out double into penalties by passing.

e.g.

East	East
♠ x x x	♠ A Q J x x
♡ A x x	♡ x x
♢ x x	♢ K J x x
♣ K Q J x x	♣ x x

West	North	East	South
1◇	2♣	Pass	Pass
Dbl*	Pass	Pass!	

West	North	East	South
1♣	1♠	Pass	Pass
Dbl*	Pass	Pass!	

Let's look at these two examples from the opener's point of view.

e.g.

West	West
♠ K J x	♠ x
♡ K Q x x	♡ A J x x
♢ K Q J x x	♢ Q x x
♣ x	♣ A K Q J x

West	North	East	South
1◇	2♣	Pass	Pass
Dbl*			

West	North	East	South
1♣	1♠	Pass	Pass
Dbl*			

On both occasions you hold a sound opening bid with a shortage in the suit overcalled plus support for the unbid suits. You will not always be dealt such ideal hands for the expected re-opening double, though. Take a look at these examples:

GENERAL PRINCIPLES
AND DISCUSSION POINTS CONTINUED

e.g.

West	West
♠ K Q x	♠ x x
♡ K J x	♡ A K Q x
◇ A x x x x x	◇ Q x
♣ x	♣ A x x x x

West	North	East	South
1◇	2♣	Pass	Pass
Dbl*			

West	North	East	South
1♣	1♠	Pass	Pass
Dbl*			

You may have to re-open with even fewer points if you think that partner is sitting over there with a good hand and just itching to take a penalty. Of course, holding a distributional hand that is totally unsuitable for defending the opponent's suit doubled, opener can always re-open the bidding with a natural call.

e.g.

West	West
♠ K Q J x x x	♠ x
♡ x	♡ K Q x x x x x
◇ K Q J x x	◇ K Q J
♣ x	♣ Q x

West	North	East	South
1♠	2♣	Pass	Pass
2◇			

West	North	East	South
1♡	1♠	Pass	Pass
2♡			

1. *Partner opens 1♣. What would you reply after an overcall of 1♠?*

Hand 1a	Hand 1b	Hand 1c
♠ 4 3 2	♠ Q J 7 5	♠ K Q J 9 8
♡ K J 6 3	♡ J 6 2	♡ 5 4
◇ Q 7 6	◇ J 6 3	◇ K 9 2
♣ 8 7 4	♣ Q 4 2	♣ 6 5 4
6 HCP	7 HCP	9 HCP

Hand 1d	Hand 1e	Hand 1f
♠ A 2	♠ K J 6 5	♠ A Q 9
♡ Q J 7 6 3	♡ Q J 3 2	♡ K J 5
◇ 8 6 3	◇ K Q J 2	◇ Q J 6 5
♣ K J 6	♣ 2	♣ J 7 6
11 HCP	13 HCP	14 HCP

2. *Partner opens 1♡. What would you reply after an overcall of 2♣?*

Hand 2a	Hand 2b	Hand 2c
♠ K 3	♠ K Q 6 5	♠ A J 9 6 2
♡ Q 7 5	♡ 9 5	♡ 6 3
◇ J 7 6 4 2	◇ Q J 7 6 5	◇ K J 7 4 2
♣ 4 3 2	♣ 4 3	♣ 2
6 HCP	8 HCP	9 HCP

Hand 2d	Hand 2e	Hand 2f
♠ J 9 8 7	♠ J 9 8	♠ Q J 6 4
♡ K 7 3	♡ A 5	♡ 2
◇ 7 6	◇ 8 6 2	◇ K Q J 7 6 2
♣ A Q 3 2	♣ A Q J 9 8	♣ A 2
10 HCP	12 HCP	13 HCP

Continued on next page – Answers on page 78

3. *You have opened 1◇. Your left-hand opponent overcalls 1♠.*
   Partner doubles. What would you rebid?

Hand 3a	**Hand 3b**	**Hand 3c**
♠ 8 7	♠ A 6 5	♠ Q J 5
♡ 3 2	♡ K J 5 4	♡ 8
◇ A K Q J 6 5	◇ K 9 7 6 3	◇ A K J 7 5
♣ 9 8 7	♣ 6	♣ J 8 7 6
10 HCP	11 HCP	12 HCP

Hand 3d	**Hand 3e**	**Hand 3f**
♠ A Q 9 7	♠ K 7	♠ J 3
♡ 5 4	♡ A J 9 7	♡ A Q 6 2
◇ K Q 8 7 6	◇ Q J 7 6 5	◇ K Q J 4 3
♠ A 9	♣ A J	♣ A Q
15 HCP	16 HCP	19 HCP

4. *You have opened 1♠. Your left-hand opponent overcalls 2♣.*
   Partner doubles. What would you rebid?

Hand 4a	**Hand 4b**	**Hand 4c**
♠ K Q J 7 6	♠ A J 6 4 3 2	♠ A K 4 3 2
♡ A 8 7 6	♡ 5	♡ 6 4
◇ J 5	◇ K 3 2	◇ K J 7 6
♣ 8 2	♣ A 4 3	♣ Q 5
11 HCP	12 HCP	13 HCP

Hand 4d	**Hand 4e**	**Hand 4f**
♠ Q 8 7 6 5	♠ A Q J 8 7	♠ A Q 6 5
♡ K Q	♡ A J 8 7	♡ A Q 3
◇ A Q	◇ K 5	◇ 9 7 5
♣ J 4 3 2	♣ 6 2	♣ A Q 8
14 HCP	15 HCP	18 HCP

Continued on next page – Answers on page 78

5. *You have opened 1♡. Your left-hand opponent overcalls 2◊.*
   Partner and right-hand opponents pass. Your call?

Hand 5a	**Hand 5b**	**Hand 5c**
♠ K J 5	♠ J 9 7 6	♠ K Q 4 3
♡ A Q 7 6 5 4	♡ A Q 7 6 5	♡ K 8 7 6 5
◊ 3	◊ 3	◊ —
♣ 9 8 7	♣ A 9 8	♣ A 8 7 6
10 HCP	11 HCP	12 HCP

Hand 5d	**Hand 5e**	**Hand 5f**
♠ A 2	♠ A Q J 6	♠ A K J 6
♡ Q 7 6 5 4	♡ K Q J 5 4	♡ A Q 9 7 5 4
◊ K Q J 8	◊ 2	◊ 3
♣ J 2	♣ A J 6	♣ K Q
13 HCP	18 HCP	19 HCP

Answers on page 78

1a	**1b**	**1c**
Dbl*	1NT	Pass
1d	**1e**	**1f**
2♡	Dbl*	3NT
2a	**2b**	**2c**
2♡	Dbl*	2♠
2d	**2e**	**2f**
Dbl*	Pass	2◇
3a	**3b**	**3c**
2◇	2♡	2♣
3d	**3e**	**3f**
1NT	3♡	4♡
4a	**4b**	**4c**
2♡	2♠	2◇
4d	**4e**	**4f**
2♠	3♡	3NT
5a	**5b**	**5c**
2♡	Dbl*	Dbl*
5d	**5e**	**5f**
Pass	Dbl*	Dbl*

CHAPTER SIX

THE UNASSUMING CUE-BID

The subject of how to respond to partner's overcall sees even the experts divided in opinion. Is a change of suit forcing, invitational or to play? What is the meaning of a jump-shift? How strong is a simple or jump-raise in partner's suit? There is clearly much to discuss.

Given that you could be facing anything from a 'good' 6-count to a top-heavy 16 HCP and a distribution that could be equally wide-ranging, it is rarely possible to gauge your side's combined assets early on in the bidding.

Your task is simple enough in that you want to investigate the correct level and strain. Indeed, if there is no immediate indication of a fit, you are wise to be cautious. If, on the other hand, your partner's overcall has struck gold, you will be aiming for a different goal.

With no further intervention from the opposition, you will probably find out everything you need to know at a reasonably safe level. Unfortunately we are not living in an ideal world and opponents have a nasty habit of interfering, leaving you with a lot less room to explore. If the auction is going to be fiercely competitive, most commonly when both sides have a strong trump fit, time and space is of the essence. Maximum co-operation will be required from partner – and that goes for both of you!

In the meantime, while you are deciding on how best to proceed following partner's overcall, have a read of the Unassuming Cue-bid convention which is designed to help you cope with two very specific hand types.

Sometimes referred to as a 'two-way cue-bid', the Unassuming Cue-bid describes a hand that is either powerful enough to want to drive to game – regardless of what you or your partner might have overcalled on – or one with at least 3-card support and 10 or more HCP.

Imagine being able to send partner a message that conveys your high-card strength and the possibility of a fit before the auction spirals out of control – sounds too good to be true!

The benefits of this gadget will be more obvious to those of you who like to play duplicate or teams bridge when you can often suffer from competitive nightmares. Now, with a wave of your magic wand your new convention will be instrumental in helping you to decide whether or not you should be defending or declaring, and will also enable you to pre-empt the auction confidently and effectively. Even your judgement in the sacrificing zone will improve as the Unassuming Cue-bid paves the way for that all-important decision: to bid or not to bid and, in my opinion, the ultimate reward for playing this system.

Time to reveal the mystery!

THE UNASSUMING CUE-BID CONVENTION

Well, er – you just bid the opponent's suit! Yes, it's that easy! The difficulty rating there is zero and it will hardly be a strain on the memory. After all, how often do you want to play in a suit that has been bid naturally by your opponents? (This is not a trick question! The answer can genuinely be found in Chapter 11!)

Time to set the scene for a recap:

1. Your left-hand opponent has started the auction with a suit opening bid.

2. Your partner overcalls in a different suit. At this stage we will assume that your right-hand opponent passes (although this is not a pre-requisite for being able to use the convention).

3. You bid your left-hand opponent's suit at the lowest available level – alerted by partner, needless to say.

THE UNASSUMING CUE-BID
CONVENTION CONTINUED

Question: What are you showing?

Answer: Either

a) A sound raise to at least three of partner's suit.
   i.e. anything from 10 upwards in terms of HCP.

 e.g.
South	West	North	East	South
♠ K 7 6	1♡	1♠	Pass	2♡*
♡ J 7				
◇ A K 6 2				
♣ 7 6 5 4				

You may be wondering why you are not making a normal raise to 3♠. Well, if you use an Unassuming Cue-bid to indicate a hand like this, you can jump to 3♠ holding something like . . .

 e.g.
South	West	North	East	South
♠ J 6 4 2	1♡	1♠	Pass	3♠*
♡ 2				
◇ K J 6 5 4				
♣ 4 3 2				

. . . gulp! (and this would be considered a good hand for the auction, believe me!) Holding a modest collection, your left-hand opponent will not be too enamoured to find that his next bid might have to be made at the four level!

THE UNASSUMING CUE-BID
CONVENTION CONTINUED

Answer: Or

b) Any hand where you have the power to insist on game, but are unsure of the correct strain or level.

e.g.

South	West	North	East	South
♠ K Q 6 5	1◇	2♣	Pass	2◇*
♡ Q J 9 8				
◇ J 5				
♣ A J 5				

Enough goodies to take-off but no idea where to land. A good time to use the magic carpet to find the right spot on this deal . . .

. . . and here's another gem of a problem:

e.g.

South	West	North	East	South
♠ 5 4	1♠	2♡	Pass	2♠*
♡ K Q 5 4				
◇ A 7 6				
♣ A K 9 8				

Anyone can bid to 4♡ with this monster but it's easy to envisage a slam. A bid of the opponent's suit here buys you valuable space to explore that possibility. At the same time your promise of a fair mitt also serves as a warning to your opponents who may be contemplating some frisky competitive activity.

THE UNASSUMING CUE-BID
CONVENTION CONTINUED

RESPONSES TO THE UNASSUMING CUE-BID

Given a free run, i.e. no further contribution from either opponent, the overcaller should respond by giving an accurate account of his assets.

There are numerous options available to you as the overcaller:

a) Rebid your own suit at the minimum level.

b) Rebid a new suit at the minimum level (i.e. a non-jump).

c) Make a jump-rebid in your own suit.

d) Rebid no-trumps.

e) Make a reverse bid or a jump-shift.

and if you're really stuck . . .

f) . . . Return the cue-bid by repeating the opponent's suit!

Facing rebids (a) or (b), the cue-bidder can stop short of game if the necessary values are clearly not present. The other responses, which show extra values, are best treated as game-forcing manoeuvres, if only for the sake of simplicity.

GENERAL PRINCIPLES
AND DISCUSSION POINTS

1. This convention combines well with a change of suit by the responder being forcing for one round.

   e.g.   (1♣) – 1♡ – (Pass) – 2◇

2. Don't forget that a jump raise in partner's suit can be very weak. Having said that, a leap to game can be a two-way shot. Maybe weak, maybe medium-strength, but basically designed to flummox your opponents and keep 'em guessing!

   e.g.   (1♡) – 1♠ – (Pass) – 4♠

3. A simple raise can be made with just 3-card support and 6-9 HCP.

   e.g.   (1♣) – 1♡ – (Pass) – 2♡
   or: (1♡) – 2◇ – (Pass) – 3◇

4. If you use the convention when you have already passed, it won't take an expert – or even a budding expert – to work out which hand-type you hold! The overcaller should use this information to maximum advantage and pre-empt the auction appropriately, according to his strength.

5. Don't forget that overcalls are expected to be good when you're vulnerable, and should be a 6-carder if made at the two level. While intervention at the one level can be made on a low point count and just a 5-card suit, overcalls at the two level should resemble an opening bid. Bear all this in mind when you are asked to evaluate your hand on the next round of the auction.

LEARNING BY EXAMPLES

1. *Your left-hand opponent opens 1◊. Partner overcalls 1♠,*
   and this is passed to you. What would you respond?

Hand 1a
♠ K 7 4
♡ 9 3 2
◊ Q 4 3 2
♣ J 8 7

6 HCP

Hand 1b
♠ Q 8 7 6 5
♡ Q 4 3
◊ 4 3
♣ Q J 5

7 HCP

Hand 1c
♠ A J 4 3 2
♡ 8
◊ 4 3
♣ K 8 7 5 2

8 HCP

Hand 1d
♠ 3 2
♡ Q 9 8 7
◊ K J 9 5
♣ A 8 2

10 HCP

Hand 1e
♠ K Q 9 7
♡ A 4 3
◊ J 8 7 6
♣ J 3

11 HCP

Hand 1f
♠ Q 2
♡ K J 9 3
◊ 8 7 6 2
♣ A K Q

15 HCP

2. *Your left-hand opponent opens 1♡. Partner overcalls 2♣, which*
   is passed to you. What would you respond?

Hand 2a
♠ A 4 3
♡ 3 2
◊ 5 4 3
♣ J 9 8 7 6

5 HCP

Hand 2b
♠ Q 3 2
♡ 7 6 5
◊ K 6 5 4
♣ Q J 6

8 HCP

Hand 2c
♠ K 6 5 4
♡ A Q 3
◊ J 9 8 7
♣ 4 3

10 HCP

Hand 2d
♠ J 6 5 4
♡ J 6 5
◊ A 4
♣ A J 7 2

11 HCP

Hand 2e
♠ Q 9 8
♡ K Q J
◊ A J 8 7
♣ 9 8 7

13 HCP

Hand 2f
♠ A K J 7
♡ 9 7
◊ A Q 4 3
♣ 6 5 4

14 HCP

Continued on next page – Answers on page 90

The Unassuming Cue-bid

Now put yourself in the overcaller's shoes . . .

3. *Your right-hand opponent opens 1♣ and you overcall a vulnerable 1♡. With no further interruptions from the opposition your partner wheels out your new convention and responds 2♣*. What do you rebid?*

Hand 3a	Hand 3b	Hand 3c
♠ 8 7 6	♠ Q 4 3	♠ 9 2
♡ A K J 9 8	♡ K 8 7 6 5 3	♡ K Q 6 5 4
◇ 8 3 2	◇ K 2	◇ A J 7 4
♣ 4 3	♣ K 5	♣ Q 2
8 HCP	11 HCP	12 HCP

Hand 3d	Hand 3e	Hand 3f
♠ A Q 9 3	♠ J 7	♠ A 2
♡ A 8 7 4 2	♡ K J 8 7 6	♡ A J 9 7 4 2
◇ 4	◇ Q 4 3	◇ A 3
♣ K 8 2	♣ A Q J	♣ J 5 4
13 HCP	14 HCP	14 HCP

Continued on next page – Answers on page 90

4. *Your right-hand opponent opens 1♠ and you overcall a non-vulnerable 2◊. Once again the opponents remain silent as your partner uses the UCB by responding 2♠*. How do you value your hand?*

Hand 4a
♠ 4 3 2
♡ K 6
◊ K J 7 5 3 2
♣ K 2

10 HCP

Hand 4b
♠ A 3
♡ 6 5
◊ A 9 7 5 4 2
♣ Q J 5

11 HCP

Hand 4c
♠ Q J 7
♡ J 5
◊ A K J 6 5 4
♣ 9 8

12 HCP

Hand 4d
♠ 8 7 6
♡ A Q J 8
◊ K Q J 9 8
♣ 2

13 HCP

Hand 4e
♠ 5
♡ J 2
◊ Q J 9 8 7 6
♣ A K Q J

14 HCP

Hand 4f
♠ 4 3 2
♡ K Q
◊ A K 7 5 3 2
♣ K 6

15 HCP

Answers on page 90

Answers to Examples on pages 86-88

1a	1b	1c
2♠	3♠	4♠

1d	1e	1f
1NT	2◊*	2◊*

2a	2b	2c
4♣	3♣	2NT

2d	2e	2f
2♡*	3NT	2♡*

3a	3b	3c
2♡	2♡	2◊

3d	3e	3f
2♠	2NT	3♡

4a	4b	4c
3◊	3◊	2NT

4d	4e	4f
3♡	3♣	3♠*

The Unassuming Cue-bid

CHAPTER SEVEN

TWO-SUITED OVERCALLS

The playing potential of your thirteen cards is measured initially by its high-card strength. Distributional features also help determine the power of a hand and if, on top of these assets, you are able to locate a trump fit . . . you're off to the races!

In competition, a two-suited hand which has at least a 5-5 distribution requires a special messaging service if it is to be described accurately. How would you bid this elegant, shapely collection following a minor-suit opening bid on your right?

♠ K Q J 7 6　♡ K Q J 7 6　◇ 8 5　♣ 4

Double? 1♠? 1♡? Imagine a bid that could convey that you held both majors, at least a 5-5, and an opening bid! Surely you'd be willing to pay me a fortune for that secret!

Still not sold on the idea? Let's go back to your present options. Once your right-hand opponent has opened the bidding, it is basically unsound to make a take-out double with an off-centre shape. A double in this position should be reserved for either three-suited hands that can tolerate any choice of trump suit in response, or a strong balanced hand with 19+ HCP, or a strong single-suited earthquake. If you conform to this definition, life will be a lot easier for you and your partner in the long run. Overcalling each suit in turn might sound like a good alternative but there's no guarantee that you will actually get a second chance to bid and, even if you do, the level may be sky high. So it's back to the drawing board.

Hopefully, I have now convinced you to adopt a two-suited gadget but once again it's confession time: you see, there are plenty of conventional aids available on the market but alas, just like any bridge player, none of them is perfect.

Ultimately it will boil down to personal choice but in the meantime you may as well be given the benefit of my experience in an attempt to guide you. Well, I've played them all, and have most recently settled on a variation of Ghestem for the 'direct' overcalling seat and Michaels Cue-bids for the 'protective' position (*see page 93 for the reason why*).

MODIFIED GHESTEM
CONVENTION

for the direct overcalling seat (2nd position)

In a nutshell:

2NT*	two lowest unbid suits.
A cue-bid of the opponent's suit *	two highest unbid suits.
3♣*	two extreme unbid suits (highest and lowest).

This is how it translates in slow motion:

2NT* **Two lowest unbid suits.**
(1♣) – 2NT* diamonds and hearts
(1◊) – 2NT* clubs and hearts
(1♡) – 2NT* clubs and diamonds
(1♠) – 2NT* clubs and diamonds

A cue-bid of the opponent's suit* **Two highest unbid suits.**
(1♣) – 2♣* hearts and spades
(1◊) – 2◊* hearts and spades
(1♡) – 2♡* diamonds and spades
(1♠) – 2♠* diamonds and hearts

3♣* **Two extreme unbid suits (highest and lowest).**
(1♣) – 3♣* diamonds and spades
(1◊) – 3♣* clubs and spades
(1♡) – 3♣* clubs and spades
(1♠) – 3♣* clubs and hearts

These overcalls are artificial and alertable

MICHAELS CUE-BIDS CONVENTION

for the protective seat (4th position)

In another nutshell:

A cue-bid of the opponent's *minor* *	both majors
A cue-bid of the opponent's *major* *	the other major and a minor

Let's see how this pans out:

(1♣) – Pass – (Pass) – 2♣*	hearts and spades
(1◇) – Pass – (Pass) – 2◇*	hearts and spades
(1♡) – Pass – (Pass) – 2♡*	spades and a minor
(1♠) – Pass – (Pass) – 2♠*	hearts and a minor

You can also include sequences which start with a suit on your left, pass from partner, and a 1NT response on your right to deliver exactly the same message: e.g. (1♡) – Pass – (1NT) – 2♡*.

All these bids are artificial and alertable.

All other bids *including* 2NT and 3♣ are *natural*.

WHY YOU SHOULD USE MICHAELS CUE-BIDS IN FOURTH POSITION

Pre-empting the auction in second seat is a good competitive ploy as it often creates difficulties for the opponents. However, the 2NT* and 3♣* overcalls in the protective seat, when valuable information has already been exchanged, are best played as natural calls. Hence the reason for varying your methods.

RESPONSES TO TWO-SUITED OVERCALLS
(MODIFIED GHESTEM
AND MICHAELS CUE-BIDS)

1. Assume that partner is at the weaker end of your agreed point range *(see Note 3, page 95)*. With the strong variety he can (and usually should) bid again.

2. If both suits are known, make a preference bid at the most appropriate level.

3. To enquire for partner's minor, in response to a Michaels cue-bid showing a major and a minor, just bid no-trumps at the lowest available level. This bid is artificial and alertable.

4. Pre-empt the auction as high as sensibly possible holding four or more of partner's suit.

5. If the conventional overcall is doubled and you have equal length in both of partner's known suits you should pass and let partner choose the trump suit.

GENERAL PRINCIPLES
AND DISCUSSION POINTS

1. Don't try to be clever by using these conventions with anything less than a 5-5 distribution. Partner will be competing on the strength of this information and will be at liberty to control the subsequent auction for your side.

2. Your two suits should pass the suit-quality test to avoid senseless penalties. Ideally that means that each of your suits should contain a couple of honour cards but on a practical level that is far too harsh a restriction. Your judgement, the prevailing vulnerability and any extra distributional features will be influencing factors on your decision to use your new toy. Remember, compete sensibly and you'll show a profit.

3. General consensus amongst the expert fraternity recommends a combination of point ranges for this convention to avoid confusion. (a) weak and strong, or (b) weak and intermediate, or (c) intermediate and strong. I believe the majority favour option (a). Having tried that style I now play option (c) and so far, so good. To show a weak two-suiter you can always enter the auction later once you've sussed out the temperature.

   Intermediate is defined as ordinary opening bid values. On that basis, you don't have to be Sherlock Holmes to work out what's required for the other strengths!

   The example hands presume you want to play it my way!

4. Partner may have announced a two-suited hand, but you may be able to suggest a good trump suit of your own. Bidding the 'fourth suit' shows a good-quality 6-card (or longer) suit and while this call is not forcing, it does show invitational values.

1. *Your right-hand opponent deals and opens 1♡.*
   Make your choice of overcall.

Hand 1a	Hand 1b	Hand 1c
♠ 3	♠ A Q 9 8 7	♠ K Q J 5 4
♡ 2	♡ 3	♡ J 3
◊ K 9 8 6 5 3	◊ 8 7	◊ A J 7 5 2
♣ A Q J 5 4	♣ K Q 9 8 7	♣ 2
10 HCP	11 HCP	12 HCP

Hand 1d	Hand 1e	Hand 1f
♠ K Q J 6 5	♠ A K Q 8 6	♠ 2
♡ 7	♡ A 8 7 6 5	♡ J 2
◊ 4	◊ 3	◊ A J 8 7 2
♣ A K 8 6 4 2	♣ 9 2	♣ A K Q 6 4
13 HCP	13 HCP	15 HCP

2. *Your right-hand opponent deals and opens 1◊.*
   Make your choice of overcall.

Hand 2a	Hand 2b	Hand 2c
♠ K J 9 6 5	♠ 3	♠ A Q 9 8 7 6
♡ A J 9 8 3	♡ K Q 6 5 4	♡ K Q 7 6
◊ —	◊ 2	◊ 4 3
♣ 6 5 4	♣ K Q 6 5 4 2	♣ 2
9 HCP	10 HCP	11 HCP

Hand 2d	Hand 2e	Hand 2f
♠ 2	♠ K J 8 6 5	♠ Q
♡ J 6 5	♡ 2	♡ A K 8 7 6
◊ K J 5	◊ K 3	◊ J 6
♣ A K Q 9 8 7	♣ A K J 7 6	♣ A Q 7 6 5
14 HCP	15 HCP	16 HCP

Continued on next page – Answers on page 100

Two-suited Overcalls

3. *Partner has overcalled 2NT to your LHO opening 1♠ call.*
   How would you respond? (1♠) – 2NT* – (Pass) – ?

Hand 3a	**Hand 3b**	**Hand 3c**
♠ 8765	♠ KQ94	♠ 2
♡ 8765	♡ 943	♡ 7642
◇ 85	◇ 532	◇ J9865
♣ 765	♣ 864	♣ A43
0 HCP	5 HCP	5 HCP

Hand 3d	**Hand 3e**	**Hand 3f**
♠ K43	♠ A87	♠ J75
♡ Q9642	♡ 8642	♡ KQ9876
◇ 654	◇ 42	◇ A3
♣ J9	♣ KQ86	♣ 98
6 HCP	9 HCP	10 HCP

4. *Partner has cue-bid 2♠ after LHO opened this suit.*
   How would you respond? (1♠) – 2♠* – (Pass) – ?

Hand 4a	**Hand 4b**	**Hand 4c**
♠ 9853	♠ 6543	♠ J654
♡ J7	♡ Q9752	♡ J43
◇ 864	◇ 9862	◇ Q5
♣ 8642	♣ —	♣ 9864
1 HCP	2 HCP	4 HCP

Hand 4d	**Hand 4e**	**Hand 4f**
♠ 2	♠ 873	♠ KQJ9
♡ J986	♡ 5	♡ 32
◇ AQ6	◇ 32	◇ Q32
♣ 86532	♣ AKQ8762	♣ KQJ9
7 HCP	9 HCP	14 HCP

Continued on next page – Answers on page 100

5. The auction has started $(1\heartsuit) - Pass - (Pass) - ?$ to you.
   It's your bid in the protective seat.

Hand 5a	Hand 5b	Hand 5c
♠ A Q J 7 6	♠ 3	♠ K Q J 7 4
♡ 3	♡ 7 6	♡ A J 7 3 2
◇ 8 6	◇ A Q J 7 6	◇ 2
♣ Q J 8 7 6	♣ K J 8 4 2	♣ J 7
10 HCP	11 HCP	12 HCP

Hand 5d	Hand 5e	Hand 5f
♠ Q J 8 7 3	♠ A K J 8 7 3	♠ Q 2
♡ 9	♡ 6 5	♡ A K 7
◇ K Q J 7 2	◇ A 4 3	◇ K Q J 6
♣ A 3	♣ Q 2	♣ A 6 3 2
13 HCP	14 HCP	19 HCP

6. Your RHO opens $1\heartsuit$. After two passes, partner 'protects' with a
   Michaels cue-bid of $2\heartsuit$: $(1\heartsuit) - Pass - (Pass) - 2\heartsuit* - (Pass) - ?$
   How would you respond?

Hand 6a	Hand 6b	Hand 6c
♠ 5 4 3	♠ 3 2	♠ J 8
♡ J 4 3 2	♡ Q 6	♡ 9
◇ Q 3 2	◇ K 5	◇ K Q 8 7 6
♣ Q 5 4	♣ Q J 10 9 8 7 6	♣ Q J 7 6 5
5 HCP	8 HCP	9 HCP

Hand 6d	Hand 6e	Hand 6f
♠ 8 6	♠ Q J 5 4	♠ K 5 4 3
♡ Q 9 5	♡ A 9 8 6	♡ A J 2
◇ A 9 4 3	◇ K 6 2	◇ 5
♣ A 9 4 3	♣ J 2	♣ A 5 4 3 2
10 HCP	11 HCP	12 HCP

Answers on page 100

BIDDING IN FOURTH SEAT – A REMINDER

Just in case you need it, here is a reminder of the requirements expected for bidding in the protective seat (as per the methods I recommended in *Bridge with Brunner – Acol bidding for Improvers*), the salient points of which are:

1NT	11-14 HCP
2NT	19-21 HCP (and a stopper in the opponent's suit)
Jump overcall	11-15 HCP Intermediate Good 6+ card suit
Double	10+ HCP with a shortage in the suit opened *or* too strong for any of the above actions

1a	1b	1c
2NT*	3♣*	2♡

1d	1e	1f
3♣*	1♠	2NT*

2a	2b	2c
2◇*	2NT*	1♠

2d	2e	2f
2♣	3♣*	2NT*

3a	3b	3c
3♣	3♣	5◇

3d	3e	3f
3◇	4♣	3♡

4a	4b	4c
3◇	4♡	3♡

4d	4e	4f
4♡	3♣	3NT

5a	5b	5c
2♡*	2◇	1♠

5d	5e	5f
2♡*	2♠	2NT

6a	6b	6c
2♠	3♣	2NT*

6d	6e	6f
2NT*	3♠	4♠

CHAPTER EIGHT

ROMAN KEY-CARD BLACKWOOD

- Have you ever gone down in a slam because you were missing an ace *and* the king of trumps?

- Have you ever missed an opportunity to bid a making slam because you knew there was an ace missing and thought the king of trumps might be missing too?

- Have you ever been afraid to go slamming because your own trump holding was particularly weak, only to find that partner held all the missing honours?

- Do you favour the Gerber 4♣* convention in auctions where you are not responding directly to a 1NT or 2NT opening bid?

If you answered 'yes' to any one of these questions, you need to think seriously about taking Roman Key-Card Blackwood (RKCB) on board. Even if you are happy with the old-fashioned version of Blackwood you already play, I hope that curiosity will get the better of you because if you want to be a serious contender for the 'budding improver' award RKCB is a 'must'.

OK, it's confession time. I played top-level bridge for the best part of twenty years before I felt confident enough even to consider changing my ace-asking methods. I now regret not having had the courage to do it earlier, because this convention has proved to be invaluable and I just can't envisage life without it. To be honest, the slam zone used to be a real weakness of mine until RKCB came to the rescue!

Like many conventions, it looks simple enough to start with – but its simplicity is quite deceptive! With numerous tomes in the bookshops on the subject, it really can be quite a frightening topic to study. However, who needs a thick book to scare you when you can read my interpretation in just a few pages – only don't turn out the lights . . . !

ROMAN KEY-CARD BLACKWOOD
CONVENTION

4NT* is still 'Blackwood' asking for aces but the reply includes a 'fifth' ace: *the king of trumps*. The four aces and the king of trumps are called 'key cards'.

5♣*   1 or 4 out of five key cards . . .
            . . . possibly the *trump queen,* too! ⎫
                                                  ⎬ *see page 104*
5◇*   0 or 3 out of five key cards . . . ⎭
            . . . possibly the *trump queen,* too!

5♡*   2 or 5 key cards without the trump queen.

5♠*   2 or 5 key cards plus the trump queen.

5NT*   2 key cards and a useful void.
            'Useful' does not include a suit
            which has been bid naturally by partner.

6 of a   1 or 3 key cards and a void in the bid suit.
new suit* (Below the agreed trump suit!)

6 of the   1 or 3 key cards
agreed   and a void in a suit ranking above
trump suit* the agreed trump suit.

Perhaps I should stop right here, because so far it's simple enough. Well, if that's what *you* want to do, see you later – but there's lots more to come!

If the key-card bidder needs more information before deciding on the best spot, there are three options:

1. ASK FOR KINGS

    A bid of 5NT* asks for the number of kings held but excludes the king of trumps as this information is already known.

    Reply: 6♣* = 0, 6◇* = 1, 6♡* = 2 , 6♠* = 3.

ROMAN KEY-CARD BLACKWOOD
CONVENTION CONTINUED

2. ASK FOR THE QUEEN OF TRUMPS

Following a 5♣* or 5◊* response, a bid of the next suit up (excluding the trump suit, which would be a sign off holding 0 or 1 key card) asks for *the queen of trumps*.

Reply:

a) Return to trump suit	No trump queen
b) 5NT*	Trump queen plus no side king
c) New suit*	Trump queen plus king of suit bid (just like a cue-bid)

3. CHECK UP ON A SIDE SUIT CONTROL

A bid of a new suit at the six level can be used to check on the control of that specific suit for the purposes of bidding a grand slam. This facility can be used before or after asking for the queen of trumps.

Reply:

a) No control	Sign off in trump suit
b) 2nd round control	Bid grand slam
c) 3rd round control	Bid new suit below trump suit

GENERAL PRINCIPLES
AND DISCUSSION POINTS

1. A fifth trump, when the asker is expecting four, counts as the trump queen.

2. A fourth trump, when the asker is known to hold six, counts as the trump queen.

3. An alternative method for replying to the king-ask is to show specific kings, i.e. bid the king(s) that you have:

    $$6\clubsuit^* = \clubsuit K \quad 6\diamondsuit^* = \diamondsuit K \quad 6\heartsuit^* = \heartsuit K \quad 6\spadesuit^* = \spadesuit K$$

4. If you want to make a jump bid above the level of 3NT to agree a minor suit as trumps, it is advisable to hold at least one key card.

5. When a minor suit has been agreed as trumps, the RKCB asker needs to hold two key cards to use the system with any degree of safety. Be especially prepared for a $5\diamondsuit^*$ response when clubs are the agreed suit!

6. Don't forget that 5NT* invites a grand slam. Therefore, this bid guarantees that the partnership already owns all five key cards and the queen of trumps.

7. An easy way to remember that you are playing the 14 – 03 version *(see page 102*)* is to recall the score for bidding and making a vulnerable major-suit slam: 1430!

8. If you have already dabbled with the alternative 30-41 response to RKCB, you may want to know why I think my version is superior. As explained in various publications by the guru of RKCB, Eddie Kantar, the asker usually holds the stronger hand. If the response to show one ace is $5\diamondsuit$, there is no room to enquire for the queen of trumps when hearts is the agreed suit. *Q.E.D.*

9. If RKCB is employed when there has clearly been no specific trump suit agreement, even by inference, the king of the last-mentioned suit becomes the 'fifth ace'.

LEARNING BY EXAMPLES

1. *Spades are trumps. What is your response to 4NT*?*

Hand 1a	Hand 1b	Hand 1c
♠ K 7	♠ A K 3 2	♠ J 7 5 3
♡ 7 6 5 4	♡ 2	♡ A 6 5
◊ K 4 3	◊ A 9 8 6 3	◊ Q 8 7 5
♣ Q J 5 3	♣ 7 6 5	♣ A 2
9 HCP	11 HCP	11 HCP

Hand 1d	Hand 1e	Hand 1f
♠ Q 8 7 5	♠ Q J 7 6 5	♠ K 9 8 7
♡ A 6 5	♡ K 3 2	♡ A 7 6
◊ J 7 5 3	◊ K 7 2	◊ A
♣ A 2	♣ Q J	♣ A 9 7 6 5
11 HCP	12 HCP	15 HCP

2. *Partner continues with 5NT*. How do you reply on each of the hands above?*

Continued on next page – Answers on page 108

HOW TO COPE
WHEN OPPONENTS INTERFERE OVER 4NT

BELOW 5 OF YOUR TRUMP SUIT = USE DOPI

Double (D̲O̲)	0 key cards
Pass (P̲I̲)	1 key card
First step	2 key cards
Second step	3 key cards
Third step	4 key cards

ABOVE 5 OF YOUR TRUMP SUIT = USE DEPO

Double (D̲E̲)	0 or 2 key cards (Even)
Pass (P̲O̲)	1 or 3 key cards (Odd)
First step	4 key cards

3. *Hearts are trumps. What is your response to 4NT*?*

Hand 3a	Hand 3b	Hand 3c
♠ J 7 5 4	♠ K Q 3	♠ A 5 4 3
♡ A K 6 5 3	♡ Q 9 8 7 6	♡ J 8 7 6
◇ 5 4 3	◇ 4 3	◇ K Q J 6 5
♣ 2	♣ K 7 5	♣ —
8 HCP	10 HCP	11 HCP

Hand 3d	Hand 3e	Hand 3f
♠ A K Q 3	♠ 8 6	♠ A 5 2
♡ A J 7 5	♡ K Q 6 5	♡ A K 7 3
◇ 9 8	◇ K 9 7 4	◇ A K 6 5
♣ 9 8 7	♣ A K J	♣ J 4
14 HCP	16 HCP	19 HCP

4. *Partner continues with 6♣*. How do you reply on each of the hands above?*

Continued on next page – Answers on page 108

Roman Key-Card Blackwood

5. *Diamonds are trumps. What is your response to 4NT*?*

Hand 5a	Hand 5b	Hand 5c
♠ K Q 3	♠ 2	♠ 8 6 5 4
♡ J 7 6 5	♡ 9 8 7 6 5	♡ 2
◊ 8 6 4 2	◊ K Q J 6	◊ A K 4 3
♣ 5 4	♣ J 3 2	♣ K 8 7 6
6 HCP	7 HCP	10 HCP

Hand 5d	Hand 5e	Hand 5f
♠ 6 5	♠ Q 9 4	♠ J 2
♡ A 8 6	♡ 6 5 4	♡ A Q J 7
◊ Q J 6 5 4	◊ A K Q 6	◊ K Q 2
♣ K Q 3	♣ Q J 5	♣ A K 6 5
12 HCP	14 HCP	20 HCP

6. *Partner continues with 5♡* over any 5♣* or 5◊* response, or 5NT* over any 5♡* or 5♠* response. Your reply on each of the hands above is?*

Answers on page 108

1a	**1b**	**1c**
5♣*	5♢*	5♡*

1d	**1e**	**1f**
5♠*	5♢*	5♣*

2a	**2b**	**2c**
6♢*	6♣*	6♣*

2d	**2e**	**2f**
6♣*	6♡*	6♣*

3a	**3b**	**3c**
5♡*	5♢*	6♣*

3d	**3e**	**3f**
5♡*	5♠*	5♣*

4a	**4b**	**4c**
7♡	7♡	7♡

4d	**4e**	**4f**
6♡	7♡	6♢*

5a	**5b**	**5c**
5♢*	5♣*	5♡*

5d	**5e**	**5f**
5♣*	5♠*	5♢*

6a	**6b**	**6c**
6♢*	5NT*	6♢*

6d	**6e**	**6f**
6♣*	6♣*	6♣*

CHAPTER NINE

SPLINTERS

If you've never heard of a Splinter bid I expect your success in the slam-bidding zone has been minimal. Any serious contender for the 'Budding Expert of the Year' award needs to have this convention in their repertoire. Let's just say it's any good bridge player's secret weapon when it comes to making decisions in the slam zone.

Originally devised by Dorothy Hayden Truscott in the '60s, the Splinter bid is a way of showing a 'negative' control, i.e. a singleton or void, whilst agreeing partner's suit as trumps.

Based on fit and distribution, rather than high cards, Splinter bids suggest slam. Pin-pointing a shortage places the rest of one's high-card goodies in the other three suits, allowing partner to assess the benefits of the combined assets for slam with the bidding still below game level.

Modern trends encourage cue-bidding sequences to introduce both negative and positive controls to the auction in economical fashion. For the most part this treatment is successful. The occasional downside often leaves partner unable to distinguish between the two types. A Splinter bid can always be recognised as a negative control because it is denoted by a jump cue-bid. As it is able to convey such a precise and important message, any problems usually associated with space-consuming bids are overwhelmingly outweighed.

The merits of this convention are clearly formidable. Let's not wait a moment longer to find out more.

SPLINTERS
CONVENTION

Defined as an 'unnecessary jump', it replaces a bid that is rarely used in response to partner's opening bid. Instead of showing a natural pre-empt, the Splinter bid is far more effectively employed to describe a hand that has *all* of these qualities:

1. Game values – 11-15 HCP.

2. A singleton or void in the suit bid.

3. Four or more of partner's suit.
   (Or three cards if partner has shown five.)

e.g.	West	East
	♠ K 3	♠ A 6 5 4
	♡ A J 10 9 8	♡ K Q 7 5
	◇ 9 5 4 3	◇ 2
	♣ A Q	♣ K 8 7 6

West	East
1♡	4◇*[1]
4NT*[2]	5♠*[3]
6♡	

[1] Splinter
[2] RKCB
[3] 2 key cards plus the queen of trumps.

It's all about having your points and shortages in the right places! With just 26 high-card points between the two hands and only one diamond loser, a small slam in hearts is an excellent contract. As you can see, the diamond shortage on this occasion works like magic!

SPLINTERS
CONVENTION CONTINUED

The news of a club shortage on this deal is anything but magical to the dealer here and thus encourages a brisk sign-off.

e.g.

West	East
♠ K 3	♠ A 6 5 4
♡ A J 10 9 8	♡ K Q 7 5
◊ 9 5 4 3	◊ K 8 7 6
♣ A Q	♣ 2

West	East
1♡	4♣*
4♡	

Even the five level could be too high. Thank goodness the brakes can be applied in the nick of time!

GENERAL PRINCIPLES
AND DISCUSSION POINTS

1. This multi-talented gadget is not just confined to a response of partner's opening bid, and can be extended to other sequences. Just look at all these positions!

   a) In response to partner's opening bid.

      e.g.   1♡ – 4◇*

   b) Following partner's response.

      e.g.   1♡ – 1♠
             4♣*

   c) Following partner's rebid.

      e.g.   1♣ – 1♡
             1♠ – 4◇*

   d) Even over partner's overcall.

      e.g.   (1♠) – 2♡ – (Pass) – 4◇*

GENERAL PRINCIPLES
AND DISCUSSION POINTS CONTINUED

A couple more rules, though . . .

2. Singleton aces do not pass the Splinter test. As partner is evaluating his hand based on the premise that all your high-card points are positioned in the other three suits, you will misrepresent the true strength of your hand if you splinter on a singleton ace. If your singleton honour is not the ace, there is unlikely to be any damage providing you exclude these points from your total.

3. I suggested a point range of 11-15 but you need to be flexible. Some 15-counts might be better described via a jump-shift if you have a good 5-carder outside the trump suit. By the same token, some 10-counts are worth game where even an 11 or 12-point hand might only merit a raise to the three level. Use your judgement.

4. Watch out for the 1♠ – 4♡* response!

5. You can also jump to 3♡* or 3♠* in response to an opening bid of 1♣ or 1◊. This bid helps the opener to estimate the true value of any high-card points held in this suit when there is a choice between game in no-trumps or a minor suit.

Losing the opportunity to make a natural, pre-emptive response in a major over partner's opening bid of 1♣ or 1◊ is no hardship. Designed to rob the opponents of bidding space, such manoeuvres are far more likely to be detrimental to your side than theirs once partner has opened the bidding.

1. *Make your response to partner's opening bid of 1♡:*

Hand 1a	Hand 1b	Hand 1c
♠ A K 4 3	♠ Q J 7 4	♠ 2
♡ K 8 6 4 3 2	♡ J 6 5 4	♡ A J 7 6 4
◇ —	◇ K 6 5 3	◇ J 4 3
♣ 9 8 7	♣ A	♣ K Q J 6
10 HCP	11 HCP	12 HCP

Hand 1d	Hand 1e	Hand 1f
♠ 9 8 6 4	♠ K Q J 6	♠ 9 7 5
♡ K Q 6 5	♡ K J 7 6	♡ K Q J 5
◇ A Q 7 3	◇ J	◇ A K Q 6 5
♣ Q	♣ K 6 5 3	♣ 2
13 HCP	14 HCP	15 HCP

2. *Make your response to partner's opening bid of 1♠:*

Hand 2a	Hand 2b	Hand 2c
♠ Q J 8 7	♠ K 9 7 6	♠ K J 7 5 4
♡ K 6	♡ A J 5	♡ 3
◇ 3	◇ J 8 6 5 4	◇ A K J 5
♣ A 8 7 5 3 2	♣ J	♣ 9 7 3
10 HCP	10 HCP	12 HCP

Hand 2d	Hand 2e	Hand 2f
♠ A Q J 7 5	♠ Q 4 3 2	♠ K Q J 8
♡ Q 3 2	♡ A K 4	♡ 8
◇ K J 7 4 3	◇ Q	◇ 7
♣ —	♣ K 7 6 3 2	♣ A K Q 8 6 5 3
13 HCP	14 HCP	15 HCP

Continued on next page – Answers on page 118

3. *Make your response to partner's opening bid of 1♣:*

Hand 3a	**Hand 3b**	**Hand 3c**
♠ 6	♠ A J 7 6 5	♠ A 9 8
♡ K J 2	♡ A	♡ 4
◊ Q J 7 6	◊ J 7 6	◊ A J 5
♣ A Q 7 6 5	♣ K 8 7 6	♣ K J 7 6 3 2
13 HCP	13 HCP	13 HCP

Hand 3d	**Hand 3e**	**Hand 3f**
♠ Q 5 4	♠ K Q 2	♠ A K Q J 5
♡ K Q J 9	♡ A J 2	♡ 5
◊ 2	◊ Q	◊ 8 6
♣ A Q 7 5 2	♣ Q 8 6 4 3 2	♣ K Q J 8 3
14 HCP	14 HCP	16 HCP

4. *Make your rebid as opener after the auction 1♡ – 1♠:*

Hand 4a	**Hand 4b**	**Hand 4c**
♠ K J 7 6	♠ Q 4 3 2	♠ A K 6 5
♡ K Q 8 7 6	♡ A 8 5 4 2	♡ A K 6 5 4 3
◊ Q 6 4	◊ 4	◊ 6 5
♣ J	♣ A K 6	♣ 2
12 HCP	13 HCP	14 HCP

Hand 4d	**Hand 4e**	**Hand 4f**
♠ K J 7 6	♠ A Q 8 7	♠ A Q J 5
♡ K Q 7 6	♡ A K 7 5 2	♡ Q J 8 7 6
◊ K Q J 4	◊ —	◊ A K 7
♣ 3	♣ Q J 7 3	♣ Q
15 HCP	16 HCP	19 HCP

Continued on next page – Answers on page 118

5. *Make your response to partner's overcall of 1♠:*
   (1♡) − 1♠ − (Pass) − ?

Hand 5a
♠ J 8 4 3 2
♡ Q J 6 5
◇ Q 3 2
♣ 6

6 HCP

Hand 5b
♠ K Q J 8 7
♡ —
◇ 9 8 7 6 5
♣ 4 3 2

6 HCP

Hand 5c
♠ A J 7
♡ K 9 8 7
◇ Q 8 6 5 4
♣ 2

10 HCP

Hand 5d
♠ K 7 6 5 4
♡ 9 8 7
◇ A
♣ K Q J 9

13 HCP

Hand 5e
♠ Q 9 8 6 4
♡ K Q J
◇ —
♣ A J 6 4 2

13 HCP

Hand 5f
♠ K J 6 2
♡ A K 6
◇ Q J 6 5 2
♣ 7

14 HCP

Answers on page 118

Splinters

1a	1b	1c
4◇*	3♡	3♠*

1d	1e	1f
4♣*	4◇*	3◇

2a	2b	2c
4◇*	3♠	4♡*!

2d	2e	2f
4♣*	4◇*	4NT*

3a	3b	3c
3♠*	1♠	3♡*

3d	3e	3f
1♡	3◇*	2♠

4a	4b	4c
2♠	3♠	4♣*

4d	4e	4f
3♠	4◇*	4♣*

5a	5b	5c
3♠	4♠	2♡*

5d	5e	5f
2♡*	4◇*	4♣*

The answers to examples (5) a-f assume you have read Chapter 6!

CHAPTER TEN

MODIFIED JACOBY 2NT

The bidding starts on your left (1♡) – Pass – (4♡) – ? and it's your turn to call. What would be your reaction holding the hand below?

♠ K Q 5 4
♡ 7
♢ K Q 8 6
♣ A 6 5 4

Budding expert or not, it's a difficult decision. If you are going to bid, then 'Double' is the obvious choice. This bid will reap dividends either when you have a fit – especially in spades – or when partner is stacked in hearts and you are able to glean a large penalty.

But hang on a minute! There's an opening bid on your left and a game-going hand on your right. That doesn't exactly leave partner with very much, except perhaps an exotic distribution. If you do call here, isn't it far more likely that your side will be taken to the cleaners? There again, a small minus score could be a worthwhile sacrifice! Decisions, decisions, decisions.

Torn in two, you elect to pass. The dummy tables the following collection and you gasp in horror!

♠ 2
♡ J 8 6 4 3 2
♢ A 5 4 3 2
♣ Q

Minus 420 points later you also notice that game in spades was cold your way. You feel cheated and humiliated as your opponents seems to have 'put one past you'.

OK. It's time to let you in on a little secret. You have been the victim of a 'sting'. Of course, you were expecting your right-hand opponent to have loads more points – but his partner wasn't! In fact it was no surprise at all. A weak, distributional hand with lots of trumps was all part of their system and it worked a treat here!

Well, I've got news for you. This style of bidding is perfectly normal these days and you can see why! It's just so effective and you know what they say? If you can't beat 'em it's time to jump on the bandwagon and join 'em.

If a direct raise to game in partner's major is going to be made with a weak hand, you will need a mechanism for showing a good hand – just like the one you were expecting to see hit the deck! Remember Oswald Jacoby, of Transfers fame? Well, he's come up trumps again!

MODIFIED JACOBY 2NT
CONVENTION

Used in direct response to partner's opening bid of 1♡ or 1♠ when:

a) you are *not* a passed hand, and
b) there has been no intervention.

A 2NT* response **SHOWS:**

1. Game values or better (usually a minimum of 12 HCP).
2. 4+ trumps.

. . . and **DENIES:**

1. The requirements for a jump-shift response.
2. The ability to make a Splinter
   (i.e. no singleton or void in the 11-15 HCP range).

In response, opener rebids as follows:

Bid game directly	Weak with no slam interest.
Bid a new suit	Shape showing. Some slam interest. (Your second suit should be at least Q-x-x-x.)
Jump in a new suit* (below game in your major)	Splinter *(see Chapter 9)*. Shows slam interest.
Rebid of your suit	Some slam interest. (No biddable second suit. No shortage.)
3NT	15-16 balanced. Not forcing.
4NT*	RKCB *(see Chapter 8)*.

GENERAL PRINCIPLES
AND DISCUSSION POINTS

1. The natural meaning of an immediate 2NT response has just gone hurtling out of the window. Does that mean goodbye to showing partner a balanced hand with 10-12 HCP? Of course not! Such an inelegant leap was always considered to be a bad move by the majority of good players so ditching that option is a welcome change.

2. 2NT still shows a balanced hand with 10-12 HCP when either you are a passed hand, or if your right-hand opponent overcalls. If neither of these situations apply and you are desperate to describe this type of hand, all you have to do is change the suit. Then, if you still think that no-trumps is a good suggestion, you can bid 2NT on the next round. Problem solved!

3. Don't forget that a direct raise to 4♡ or 4♠ without intervention shows a very weak hand.

   e.g.
              ♠ J 8 7 6 4
              ♡ K 5 4 3 2
              ◊ 3 2
              ♣ 3

   Raise an opening bid of 1♡ or 1♠ to game!

4. Sometimes the opener has a choice between showing a second suit or making a Splinter bid in response to 2NT. Information on both counts is likely to be useful, so it's up to you to choose. Perhaps the Splinter hints more strongly at slam prospects, as it takes up a lot of space.

1. *Partner opens 1♡ in first position. Your right-hand opponent passes. How would you respond?*

Hand 1a	Hand 1b	Hand 1c
♠ K Q 7 6 5	♠ A 4	♠ K 8 7
♡ A K 6 4	♡ K Q J 5	♡ J 6 5 4 3
◇ 3 2	◇ Q 8 7 6 5 4	◇ A Q 3
♣ 3 2	♣ 3	♣ K 6
12 HCP	12 HCP	13 HCP

Hand 1d	Hand 1e	Hand 1f
♠ Q 8	♠ A J 6 5	♠ A K J 7 6
♡ A 9 4 3	♡ K J 6 3	♡ A K 7 3
◇ 8 7	◇ 6	◇ 9 7
♣ A K 9 8 7	♣ A J 8 7	♣ 5 3
13 HCP	14 HCP	15 HCP

2. *Same as above but this time partner opens 1♠.*

Hand 2a	Hand 2b	Hand 2c
♠ K J 7 6 5 4	♠ Q J 7 5	♠ A K Q 2
♡ 8 7	♡ 3	♡ K 5 4 3
◇ 3 2	◇ K J 7 5 3	◇ Q 2
♣ K 7 6	♣ Q J 5	♣ 9 6 2
7 HCP	10 HCP	14 HCP

Hand 2d	Hand 2e	Hand 2f
♠ A K 7 6	♠ K Q 8 2	♠ A 7 6 5
♡ 9 8	♡ J 5 4	♡ A J
◇ 4	◇ A 4 3	◇ J 8 7 6 5
♣ A K J 7 6 5	♣ A Q 2	♣ A K
15 HCP	16 HCP	17 HCP

Continued on next page – Answers on page 126

3. *You opened 1♡ first position. Partner has used the conventional Jacoby 2NT response. What would you rebid?*

Hand 3a	Hand 3b	Hand 3c
♠ K 5	♠ 8 7	♠ 8 6
♡ Q J 8 6 4 2	♡ A Q 7 5 3	♡ A Q J 5 4
◊ 2	◊ K Q J 3 2	◊ 8 2
♣ K Q J 5	♣ 2	♣ A J 8 6
12 HCP	12 HCP	12 HCP

Hand 3d	Hand 3e	Hand 3f
♠ K 7 5	♠ A K 5	♠ K Q J 6
♡ K Q J 6 5 4	♡ A J 8 2	♡ A K 9 7 4 2
◊ A 4	◊ J 8 6	◊ A 5
♣ 8 5	♣ Q 4 2	♣ 6
13 HCP	15 HCP	17 HCP

4. *Same as above but this time you have opened 1♠.*

Hand 4a	Hand 4b	Hand 4c
♠ K J 8 5 2	♠ Q 5 4 3 2	♠ K Q J 5 3
♡ A K J 6	♡ J 7 5 2	♡ A K 5
◊ 4 3	◊ A J	◊ 7
♣ 8 7	♣ K Q	♣ J 8 7 6
12 HCP	13 HCP	14 HCP

Hand 4d	Hand 4e	Hand 4f
♠ Q J 6 4	♠ A J 8 5 4 2	♠ A K 7 6 5
♡ Q 9 8	♡ A 4 3	♡ A 4
◊ K Q 3	◊ K Q	◊ K Q J 6
♣ A Q 3	♣ Q 3	♣ 3 2
16 HCP	16 HCP	17 HCP

Continued on next page – Answers on page 126

Modified Jacoby 2NT

5. *Now let's have a look at a few 10-12 HCP hands which are denied the 'natural' response of 2NT when partner opens 1♠:*

Hand 5a	**Hand 5b**	**Hand 5c**
♠ 6 5	♠ J 8 5	♠ 9 3
♡ K J 8 5	♡ Q 5 3 2	♡ J 9 7 3
◊ Q J 7	◊ K 9 2	◊ A K 8 2
♣ K 9 4 3	♣ A 3 2	♣ K 3 2
10 HCP	10 HCP	11 HCP

Hand 5d	**Hand 5e**	**Hand 5f**
♠ Q 5 3	♠ A Q 9	♠ 8 7 6
♡ A J 4	♡ J 8 4	♡ A 6 5
◊ Q J 8 2	◊ K 6 2	◊ A 8 6 4
♣ J 5 3	♣ Q 8 7 6	♣ K J 8
11 HCP	12 HCP	12 HCP

Answers on page 126

1a	**1b**	**1c**
2NT*	4♣*	2NT*

1d	**1e**	**1f**
2NT*	4◇*	2♠

2a	**2b**	**2c**
4♠	3♠	2NT*

2d	**2e**	**2f**
3♣	2NT*	2NT*

3a	**3b**	**3c**
4◇*	4♣*	3♣

3d	**3e**	**3f**
3♡*	3NT	4NT*

4a	**4b**	**4c**
3♡	4♠	4◇*

4d	**4e**	**4f**
3NT	3♠*	3◇

5a	**5b**	**5c**
2♣	2♣!	2◇

5d	**5e**	**5f**
2◇	2♣	2◇

SECTION THREE

TREATMENTS

CHAPTER ELEVEN

BIDDING
THE OPPONENT'S SUIT

Acol thrives on being a natural system. Bidding suits that are at least four cards long, therefore, is the usual way to go about describing your hand. Interference from the opposition, however, often stems the normal flow of the auction and is particularly unwelcome when it deprives you of the luxury of expressing your hand naturally. But as the saying goes, when one door closes another one opens.

Opponent's overcalls can actually be incredibly helpful on occasions. Whether you end up as the declarer or a defender, it is routine to take advantage of any information received during a competitive auction. Why not extend this strategy to assist you during the bidding too?

If you have ever felt intimidated by the opposition's entrance into the bidding, you are now commanded to greet them with open arms! For a start, the ability to double is automatically unleashed when the enemy intrude – definitely good news! This dynamic element has already been detailed in my book for *Improvers*, hence there's no need to elaborate here.

So, what is this chapter going to be all about? It's time to introduce you to the 'Genie of the cue-bidding lamp', who only appears when the opposition make competitive noises. After all, you can't *bid the opponent's suit* until they have bid it first! Oh, and no prizes for guessing how many wishes you will be able to make!

BIDDING THE OPPONENT'S SUIT TREATMENT

Common to all three wishes:

a) The cue-bid of the opponent's suit is made at the most economical level (often referred to as a 'low-level' cue-bid) and can be made at any stage of the auction.
b) The cue-bid promises the values for game opposite whatever partner has shown to-date.
c) The cue-bid should not be used if there is a more descriptive or sensible choice available.
d) The cue-bid asks partner to respond with some useful information. Priorities differ according to whether partner's opening bid was a suit or 1NT.

WISH 1.   A cue-bid of the opponent's suit . . .
after your partner has opened with a suit bid.

Not to be confused with the Unassuming Cue-bid used after partner has overcalled *(as described in Chapter 6)*, this style of cue-bid is used after one of you has opened the auction with one of a suit.

e.g.

        ♠ 6 5
        ♡ A K Q 6 5
        ◇ Q J 4
        ♣ J 7 5

Partner opens 1♠ and your right-hand opponent overcalls 2♣. You make the obvious response of 2♡ which elicits a 2♠ rebid from partner. What now? You have already shown your 5-card heart suit, you have no primary spade support and you do not have a stopper in the opponent's suit, yet you have enough high-card points to insist on playing in game. Now, where's that genie?

1♠ – (2♣) – 2♡ – (Pass)
2♠ – (Pass) – 3♣*

BIDDING THE OPPONENT'S SUIT
TREATMENT CONTINUED

Also called a Directional Asking Bid (DAB) this cue-bid could have been made a round earlier:

e.g.
$$♠ K Q 3$$
$$♡ A K 4$$
$$◊ 5 4 3 2$$
$$♣ J 8 6$$

This time a two-level overcall in diamonds after partner has opened 1♠ creates an awkward response for you. Summon the genie and make a wish.

1♠ – (2◊) – 3◊*

WISH 2.   A cue-bid of the opponent's suit . . .
after your partner has opened 1NT.

While holding stoppers in all four suits is not a pre-requisite for opening and rebidding no-trumps, it is, nevertheless, something you are presumed to have.

That said, your partner opens 1NT and those pesky opponents deny you the chance to use the Stayman 2♣ convention by overcalling 2◊. Hmmm, I wonder if that genie is busy?

e.g.
$$♠ Q J 5 4$$
$$♡ A J 8 2$$
$$◊ J 6 5$$
$$♣ A 2$$

Well, he's available if you have game points and at least one 4-card major. Good man! It's 3◊* to the rescue and it does *not* – and I repeat *not* – ask for a diamond stopper!

1NT – (2◊) – 3◊*

BIDDING THE OPPONENT'S SUIT
TREATMENT CONTINUED

WISH 3.   A cue-bid of the opponent's suit . . .
                   after your partner has made a take-out double.

If you are responding to a take-out double, you are clearly expecting
partner to have the 'ideal' shape for this call, i.e. a shortage in the bid
suit, support for the other three (hopefully a perfect 4-4-4-1 shape)
and opening-bid values. Dreams, however, can easily be shattered
when you make a bid that anticipates an 8-card trump fit, but finds
partner tabling only three cards in trumps to go with your four.

e.g.
                         ♠ Q 8 5 2
                         ♡ A K J 3
                         ◊ K 9 8
                         ♣ 6 5

Partner doubles the opening bid of 1◊ on your left and it's up to
you to divine the correct game after RHO passes. Do you plump
for 4♡ or 4♠? How are you going to choose? Does everything
depend on the strength of your suits or just the mood you're in?
Surely you'd prefer a second opinion before making a decision!

Guess who might be able to help you! If you bid 2◊, your wish will
come true. When partner holds something like . . .

                         ♠ A K 9 4
                         ♡ 9 8 7
                         ◊ Q 2
                         ♣ A Q J 2

. . . you'll be glad you went to the trouble. Note that on this
occasion the cue-bid was not used to ask for a diamond stopper.
Rather, it put the ball back in partner's court as far as choosing a
suit was concerned.

(1◊) – Dbl – (Pass) – 2◊*
(Pass) – 2♠ – (Pass) – 4♠

BIDDING THE OPPONENT'S SUIT
TREATMENT CONTINUED

But the cue-bid of the opponent's suit can be just as useful in a similar situation when you have even greater ambitions:

e.g.
                ♠ K 6
                ♡ A 3 2
                ◊ 3 2
                ♣ A K J 7 5 3

It would be easy enough to insist on a club game but the slam zone is also beckoning. By bidding the opponent's suit first and then mentioning your clubs, you can explore this possibility without risk.

(1◊) – Dbl – (Pass) – 2◊*
(Pass) – 2♠ – (Pass) – 3♣ . . . forcing!

GENERAL PRINCIPLES
AND DISCUSSION POINTS

1. The meaning of a low-level cue-bid differs according to whether partner has opened 1NT, one of a suit, or made a take-out double.

2. Just another reminder that these cue-bids are best played as game-forcing manoeuvres. Once employed, the 'Principle of Fast Arrival' *(see NOTE on next page)* kicks in to help you distinguish between hands where you may have slam potential and those where you have anything but.

3. If you follow all the rules, you can't go too far wrong. After all, how often will you actually want to play in a suit that has been bid naturally by your opponents? What, never? Well, hardly ever! Sorry! Here is an exception!

   Look at this auction carefully:

South	West	North	East	South
♠ K 7 6	1◇	Pass	1♡	Pass
♡ A K J 6 5 4	2◇	Pass	Pass	?
◇ Q 2				
♣ 6 5				

As South, you behaved impeccably by passing on the first round when your right-hand opponent picked off your best suit. Does that mean you have to stay silent forever? The answer to that depends on the level of the auction when it next comes round to you and the combined strength of the two hands which are surrounding your hand.

The bidding here marks partner with some points, so your protective instincts should be taking over. Surely a heart contract is beckoning despite the known adverse trump break. In fact, that knowledge might work in your favour as declarer. Anyway, it's natural to bid 2♡ here – in all senses of the word!

Bidding the Opponent's Suit

GENERAL PRINCIPLES
AND DISCUSSION POINTS CONTINUED

4. Remember to be alert – and alert!

5. I expect you could do with seeing a few more examples in action before testing yourself, so please turn to the next page.

NOTE

The 'Principle of Fast Arrival' refers directly to the situation where both partners know that their combined hands contain enough points for game but game has not yet been reached.

As neither player can stop short of game, a *slow* approach suggests slam posibilities, whereas getting to game *quickly* ('fast-arrival') implies no extra values.

1. You are East and partner opens the bidding.

East	West	North	East	South
♠ 7 6 5	1♡	1♠	2♣	Pass
♡ Q 2	2♡	Pass	?	
◇ A J 7 4				
♣ A K 7 6				

Bid **2♠** – requesting a stop for no-trumps.

Although a bid of 3◇ would also be forcing to game, it would show a more distributional hand.

2. You are East and partner opens the bidding.

East	West	North	East	South
♠ A 3 2	1◇	2♡	?	
♡ 6 2				
◇ A J 4 3 2				
♣ K J 2				

Bid **3♡** – requesting a stop for no-trumps.

There is a strong inference here that you will have a fit in partner's suit – else, why did you not make a natural call?

3. You are East and partner opens the bidding.

East	West	North	East	South
♠ K Q J 7	1NT	2♡	?	
♡ 4				
◇ K 5 4 3				
♣ A 9 8 3				

Bid **3♡** – Staymanic.

After a 1NT opener it is presumed that you have all suits guarded. Therefore, a cue-bid is looking for a fit – usually with one or both majors.

4. You are East and left-hand opponent opens the bidding.

East	West	North	East	South
♠ K J 8 7				1◇
♡ A J 4 3	Dbl	Pass	?	
◇ Q 9 2				
♣ Q 5				

Bid 2◇! – Ask partner to pick a suit.

It cannot be natural. If you held a strong hand with diamonds you could have passed the double for penalties or responded in no-trumps. This cue-bid passes the ball back to partner as well as showing a good hand.

5. You are East and left-hand opponent opens the bidding.

East	West	North	East	South
♠ K Q J 7 6 5				1♣
♡ A 3	Pass	1♠	Pass	2♣
◇ Q 2	Pass	Pass	?	
♣ J 3 2				

Bid 2♠ – Natural!

Strong hands without spades would have competed earlier.

6. You are East and you open the bidding.

East	West	North	East	South
♠ K 7			1♣	1♡
♡ 3 2	1♠	2♡	?	
◇ A Q 2				
♣ A K Q J 9 8				

Bid 3♡ – requesting a stop for no-trumps.

1. *Partner opens 1NT. Your RHO overcalls 2◊. Your bid?*
   1NT – (2◊) – ?

Hand 1a	**Hand 1b**	**Hand 1c**
♠ J 4 3	♠ 7 6	♠ A K J 7
♡ K 7 6	♡ A 9 7 6	♡ K 9 7 4
◊ J 7 6 5	◊ K Q J 6	◊ 6 5 4
♣ A 6 5	♣ 8 3 2	♣ 4 3
9 HCP	10 HCP	11 HCP

Hand 1d	**Hand 1e**	**Hand 1f**
♠ A K 4	♠ K Q 9 6	♠ 8 4
♡ Q 6 5	♡ K Q 5 4	♡ A Q J 3
◊ 9 8 7	◊ J 2	◊ K 9 4
♣ K J 7 5	♣ Q 9 8	♣ A 8 7 6
13 HCP	13 HCP	14 HCP

Continued on next page – Answers on page 142

Bidding the Opponent's Suit

2. *Partner opens 1♡. Your RHO overcalls 2♣ and you respond 2◇.*
   Partner rebids 2♡. What would you bid now?
   1♡ – (2♣) – 2◇ – (Pass)
   2♡ – (Pass) – ?

Hand 2a
♠ Q 5 4
♡ J 8
◇ K Q J 6 5
♣ 4 3 2

9 HCP

Hand 2b
♠ Q 5 4
♡ J 8 4
◇ K Q J 6 5
♣ J 7

10 HCP

Hand 2c
♠ J 8 7
♡ 3 2
◇ K Q J 6 5
♣ A J 7

12 HCP

Hand 2d
♠ K 8 7
♡ A 5
◇ A Q 6 4 3
♣ 8 7 6

13 HCP

Hand 2e
♠ A Q 8
♡ 7 6
◇ Q 9 7 4 2
♣ K Q 2

13 HCP

Hand 2f
♠ A Q J
♡ K 7
◇ A J 8 7 6 5
♣ 3 2

15 HCP

Continued on next page – Answers on page 142

3. *Partner opens 1◇. Your RHO overcalls 1♠ and you respond 2♣.*
   Partner rebids 2◇. What would you bid now?
   1◇ – (1♠) – 2♣ – (Pass)
   2◇ – (Pass) – ?

Hand 3a
♠ 5 3 2
♡ K Q J
◇ J 2
♣ Q 6 5 4 3

9 HCP

Hand 3b
♠ J 7 6
♡ Q 9 3
◇ 2
♣ A K 8 7 6 5

10 HCP

Hand 3c
♠ 8 6 2
♡ A J 6
◇ Q J 6
♣ K 8 7 6

11 HCP

Hand 3d
♠ K Q 3
♡ Q 3 2
◇ K 8
♣ J 8 6 5 3

11 HCP

Hand 3e
♠ 5 4 3
♡ A Q 7
◇ 7
♣ A Q J 4 3 2

13 HCP

Hand 3f
♠ J 8
♡ K J 8
◇ A 5 4
♣ K Q 6 5 4

14 HCP

Continued on next page – Answers on page 142

4. *Your LHO opens 1♣ and partner makes a take-out double.*
    What would you reply after your RHO passes?
    (1♣) – Dbl – (Pass) – ?

Hand 4a
♠ K J 8 7 6
♡ Q 6 5 4
◇ J 7
♣ Q 3

9 HCP

Hand 4b
♠ 5 4
♡ J 5
◇ A 5 4 3
♣ K Q J 9 8

11 HCP

Hand 4c
♠ Q J 8 7 6
♡ Q J 8 7 6
◇ 4
♣ A Q

12 HCP

Hand 4d
♠ K 9 8 7
♡ Q 8 7 6
◇ A Q 3
♣ Q 3

13 HCP

Hand 4e
♠ J 4 3
♡ A 9 8 7 6 5
◇ Q
♣ A K 5

14 HCP

Hand 4f
♠ A K Q 7 6 5
♡ 5 4
◇ A Q 3
♣ 9 8

15 HCP

Answers on page 142

Answers to Examples on pages 138-141

1a	1b	1c
Pass	Dbl	2NT

1d	1e	1f
3NT	3◊*	3◊*

2a	2b	2c
Pass	3♡	2NT

2d	2e	2f
3♣*	3NT	3♣*

3a	3b	3c
Pass	3♣	3◊

3d	3e	3f
2NT	2♠*	2♠*

4a	4b	4c
2♠	Pass	2♣*

4d	4e	4f
2♣*	4♡	2♣*

Bidding the Opponent's Suit

CHAPTER TWELVE

THE FORCING 2NT REBID

Your elementary knowledge of the Acol system should tell you that opener's rebid in the sequence 1♡ – 2♣ – 2NT indicates 15-16 high-card points and that the responder required at least 9 HCP to introduce a new suit at the two level.

If I was given £1 for each time I was asked why it is not correct to rebid 3NT holding 16 HCP when partner has promised at least 9 HCP I'd be a very rich woman. But it's not easy convincing pupils that even though one member of the partnership knows that the combined requisite points for game are present, it is normal to make a technically non-forcing rebid. It's tough being a bridge teacher.

So, how do I answer that old chestnut of a problem? Your partner has opened the bidding and you hold *exactly* 9 HCP. Assuming that you can neither introduce a new suit at the one level, nor support partner's suit, what are your choices?

You can respond 1NT to show 6-9 HCP. You can also change the suit at the two level to show 9 or more HCP. There is a clear overlap when you have exactly 9, so what will influence your decision? The answer simply depends on whether you have a 5-card suit. This lone factor allows you to distinguish between a good 9-point hand and a bad 9-point hand. A hand which contains 9 HCP and a 5-card suit is surely worth 10 HCP. Now then, when did you last pass a 2NT rebid by partner holding 10 HCP? I rest my case.

I'm sure you are eager to find out where I'm heading. Well, if 2NT is *never* going to be passed, why not label it as a forcing bid and include the 17-19 HCP zone too? This leaves you with tons more room to explore for the best contract. Let's look at the benefits of playing a FORCING 2NT REBID after a change of suit at the two level in more detail.

THE FORCING 2NT REBID TREATMENT

Using the sequence originally mentioned as an example, 2NT now shows 15-19 HCP:

e.g.	West	West	East
	♠ K 8 6	1♡	2♣
	♡ K Q J 6 5	?	
	◇ A 3		
	♣ K J 3		

A few minutes ago this balanced hand would have warranted an inelegant leap to 3NT missing a possible 5-3 heart fit. Imagine partner holding something like . . .

East
♠ A 5 4
♡ A 9 8
◇ 8 7
♣ Q 9 8 7 6

. . . and you would be kissing goodbye to a plus score having missed the 4♡ boat!

THE FORCING 2NT REBID
TREATMENT CONTINUED

Now bid these two hands again playing the forcing 2NT rebid convention.

West	East
West	**East**
♠ K 8 6	♠ A 5 4
♡ K Q J 6 5	♡ A 9 8
◇ A 3	◇ 8 7
♣ K J 3	♣ Q 9 8 7 6

West	East
West	**East**
1♡	2♣
2NT	3♡
4♡	

With room for responder to show delayed major-suit support at the three level the partnership is easily able to identify the heart game and land safely.

THE FORCING 2NT REBID
TREATMENT CONTINUED

The luxury of having an extra level to explore benefits slam
bidding too. After opening 1◊ with something like:

West
♠ K 6 3
♡ A Q 2
◊ K J 7 4 3
♣ A Q

the previously routine 3NT rebid over 2♣ would have resulted in
missing a rather good slam opposite, say:

East
♠ A 2
♡ 8 7 6
◊ A 2
♣ K J 6 5 3 2

But who could blame partner for not continuing the auction here?
On another occasion the opener might have held:

West
♠ K Q J
♡ K Q J
◊ Q 8 7 6 5
♣ A 3

and even the four level could be too high!

THE FORCING 2NT REBID
TREATMENT CONTINUED

Following a 2NT rebid there are advantages too for the responder who can now utilise the space at the three level:

e.g.	East	West	East
	♠ 2	1♠	2♡
	♡ A Q J 7 6	2NT	3◊
	◊ K Q 7 4		
	♣ 7 6 5		

promising a 5-4 distribution.

e.g.	East	West	East
	♠ J 7 5	1♡	2♣
	♡ 5	2NT	3♣
	◊ A J 6		
	♣ A K J 8 6 3		

showing interest in a club game or slam.

Surely, any gadget that can improve your chances of getting to the best contract has to be worth contemplating and it's just so easy to remember!

GENERAL PRINCIPLES
AND DISCUSSION POINTS

1. One of the most interesting side effects of playing this treatment is the release of the 3NT rebid. Why not use it to show 4-card support for partner's minor and a maximum 18 or 19 HCP?

e.g.
West	West	East
♠ K Q J 6	1♠	2◇
♡ K J 6	3NT	
◇ K J 6 5		
♣ A 3		

. . . and leave the decision to partner!

As you can see my preference for opening the higher ranking of two 4-card suits often sees partner responding in your second suit at the two level. While my advice on these occasions is to suppress the minor-suit fit in favour of expressing your balanced hand there will be, needless to say, times when this action will not get you the best result.

The alternative option of supporting partner is not the answer because (a) partner will expect you to be at least a 5-4 shape and (b) you will have to bypass 3NT in order to show 16 or more HCP.

2. Going back to the beginning of this chapter we discussed your options as responder holding exactly 9 HCP. As opener is going to make a game-forcing 2NT rebid with as few as 15 HCP and a balanced hand, it is imperative that you stick to the rules and keep your two-level responses up to scratch.

1. *You open 1♡. Partner responds 2◊. What would you rebid?*

Hand 1a	Hand 1b	Hand 1c
♠ Q J 3	♠ A K J 7	♠ K 8 7
♡ K J 7 5	♡ A J 7 6	♡ A K Q J 4
◊ J 7 5 3	◊ 5 4	◊ 9 5 4
♣ A K	♣ Q 3 2	♣ K 4
15 HCP	15 HCP	16 HCP

Hand 1d	Hand 1e	Hand 1f
♠ Q 6	♠ A K	♠ A K 2
♡ K Q 5 4 3	♡ J 8 7 6	♡ J 8 7 6
◊ A 2	◊ A Q 5 4	◊ A Q 5
♣ K Q J 8	♣ A 5 4	♣ A 5 4
17 HCP	18 HCP	18 HCP

2. *You open 1♠. Partner responds 2♣. What would you rebid?*

Hand 2a	Hand 2b	Hand 2c
♠ A Q J 7 6	♠ A Q J 7 6 5	♠ K Q J 6
♡ A J 6	♡ A J 6	♡ J 6
◊ 3 2	◊ 3 2	◊ A Q 3
♣ K 6 5	♣ K J	♣ K 6 3 2
15 HCP	16 HCP	16 HCP

Hand 2d	Hand 2e	Hand 2f
♠ K Q J 6	♠ A K 4 3 2	♠ J 8 7 6 5
♡ K 9	♡ K Q 6 3	♡ Q J 6
◊ A Q 3	◊ 6	◊ A K Q
♣ K 6 3 2	♣ A J 8	♣ A Q
18 HCP	17 HCP	19 HCP

Continued on next page – Answers on page 152

3. *Partner opens 1♠. You responded 2♡.*
   Make your next response after partner rebids 2NT.

Hand 3a	Hand 3b	Hand 3c
♠ Q J 7	♠ 3	♠ 8 7
♡ K Q J 5 4	♡ A Q J 9 8 7	♡ A K 9 8 7
◇ 9 8 7	◇ Q 7 6	◇ 2
♣ 3 2	♣ 4 3 2	♣ Q J 8 7 6
9 HCP	9 HCP	10 HCP

Hand 3d	Hand 3e	Hand 3f
♠ 4	♠ A 9 2	♠ 8
♡ A J 6 4 2	♡ Q J 8 4 2	♡ A K 9 7 5 3 2
◇ 9 8 7 6	◇ A J 6	◇ K Q 3
♣ K Q J	♣ 8 5	♣ J 3
11 HCP	12 HCP	13 HCP

Continued on next page – Answers on page 152

4. *Partner opens 1♡. You responded 2◊.*
   Make your next response after partner rebids 2NT?

Hand 4a	Hand 4b	Hand 4c
♠ K J 6	♠ A 4	♠ A J 6
♡ 4 3	♡ Q 7 5	♡ 4 3 2
◊ A J 6 4 2	◊ Q 8 7 6 5	◊ K 9 8 6
♣ 4 3 2	♣ J 7 4	♣ Q 3 2
9 HCP	9 HCP	10 HCP

Hand 4d	Hand 4e	Hand 4f
♠ 8 6 4	♠ K 8 7	♠ Q J 7
♡ —	♡ K 2	♡ A 2
◊ K Q J 5 4	◊ A Q 9 8 7 6	◊ A J 4 3 2
♣ A Q 8 6 3	♣ 8 7	♣ 7 6 5
12 HCP	12 HCP	12 HCP

5. *On the hands above, partner opens 1♡. You responded 2◊.*
   Make your next response after partner rebids 3NT.

Answers on page 152

1a	1b	1c
2NT	2NT	2NT

1d	1e	1f
3♣	3NT*	2NT

2a	2b	2c
2NT	3♠	2NT

2d	2e	2f
3NT*	3♡	2NT

3a	3b	3c
3♠	4♡	3♣

3d	3e	3f
3NT	3♠	3♡

4a	4b	4c
3NT	3♡	3NT

4d	4e	4f
3♣	3♢	3NT

5a	5b	5c
Pass	Pass	Pass

5d	5e	5f
4♣	4♢	4♢

CHAPTER THIRTEEN

TRIAL BIDS

Getting to game with a combined total of 25 high-card points between the two hands is routine procedure for most bridge partnerships. If you are heading for 3NT, this is regarded as an essential quantity when both hands are balanced.

By contrast, declaring in a trump suit with a highly distributional hand it is possible to produce a mountain of tricks despite having very little in the way of high-card goodies.

Even holding a moderately-shaped hand, I'm sure that you have often been frustrated to find partner tabling just the right cards to make the game you so studiously avoided after discovering you had insufficient power. This common scenario occurs when the combination of distribution and honour cards between the two hands are a perfect match. Without the mechanism to look for that ideal hand which will complement your own, opportunities will always slip through the bidding net.

"If only I had known that you held the ace of spades," or "if only I had known that you held a singleton heart," are typical cries when chances have been missed. If only *you* had known about the magic ingredient that is obviously lacking in your language of bidding! The answer to the mystery of how to locate successful low point-count games is simply the TRIAL BID.

TRIAL BIDS
TREATMENT

When a *major* suit is raised from the one level to the two level, the responder's hand is clearly defined. He has 6-9 HCP and 4-card support.

The opening bidder's hand can be divided into three categories when it is not balanced: 'small' (up to 15 HCP), 'medium' (16-18 HCP) and 'large' (19 HCP). Holding the 'small' hand opener passes. Holding the 'large' hand opener duly bids game. For the most part these two actions are normal and get you favourable results.

When you have a 'medium-strength' hand, you have a different mission. Previously, you focused on getting to game only when facing a maximum raise, i.e. 8-9 HCP, on the assumption that this was the pre-requisite for making ten tricks. Your invitational message was conveyed by re-bidding the agreed trump suit at the three level. However, as any budding expert must surely know, success does not necessarily depend on your combined quantity of points. Sometimes just a few will do – but only if they are in just the right places – as the Trial Bid convention will demonstrate.

TRIAL BIDS
TREATMENT CONTINUED

1. TRIAL BIDS MADE BY THE OPENER

West
♠ A Q J 8 7
♡ A 2
◇ J 2
♣ A 9 8 7

The auction starts 1♠ – 2♠. An invitational raise to 3♠ with this 16-point hand would remain the final contract if partner is holding a meagre 6 or 7 HCP. Not the best outcome here, as partner tables:

East
♠ K 10 9 6
♡ 6 5 4 3
◇ 7 6 5
♣ K 2

Two club ruffs in dummy wrap up the contract – a pretty good one by anyone's standards. Yet, with only a combined 22 HCP you would not normally want to be in game, let alone expect to make it.

Include the 'long-suit trial bid' in your system and you will be able to reach these games with well-fitting hands without needing any luck or guesswork. Bidding a new suit after a *major* has been supported at the two level asks partner to evaluate his holding in that suit for game prospects. Here, you would choose to bid 3♣. With two or fewer losers in that suit, he should bid game even when minimum. Exchange responder's clubs and hearts, however, and the trial bid would elicit a prompt sign off in 3♠.

Without specific help in the suit requested, responder should still accept the game try when he holds maximum points. No change there then. The bonus lies simply in being able to highlight a second, long suit (3 or more cards) where partner might be able to reduce most of your expected losers. Consider the next example.

TRIAL BIDS
TREATMENT CONTINUED

West
♠ 6
♡ A K Q 8 4
◊ 6 5 4
♣ A K 4 3

You open 1♡ which is raised to 2♡. As your club suit is reasonably robust, your attention turns to the diamond suit where you have the bulk of your losers.

Now put yourself in the responder's shoes:

East
♠ Q J 9
♡ J 7 6 5
◊ 8 7 2
♣ Q 6 5

A swift rejection of the game try sees you stopping safely at the three level. Switch responder's spades and diamonds around, though, and it's a completely different story. The appraisal of your diamond holding should now persuade you to bid the game.

The principle of introducing a new suit after a *major* suit has been agreed should never lead to confusion, and is easily recognisable. After all, just how many fits are you looking for?

These game tries are not confined to the opening bidder either. Consider all situations where a *major*-suit game depends on discovering your total points or assistance in a particular suit and you have the answer.

TRIAL BIDS
TREATMENT CONTINUED

2. TRIAL BIDS MADE BY THE RESPONDER

East
♠ K Q 8 7 6
♡ J 6
◇ K 3
♣ Q 4 3 2

Partner opens 1♡ and raises your 1♠ response to 2♠. Time to wheel out the 3♣ trial bid and get to game when:

West
♠ A J 4 2
♡ A 9 8 7 5
◇ A 4
♣ 6 5

goes down in dummy. But it would be necessary to apply the brakes with the following selection:

West
♠ 10 9 5 4
♡ A K Q 3 2
◇ Q
♣ J 8 7

TRIAL BIDS
TREATMENT CONTINUED

3. TRIAL BIDS MADE BY THE OVERCALLER

Your overcall of 1♡ over 1♣ elicits a simple raise from partner.

♠ J765
♡ AK6432
◇ 8
♣ AJ

Only 13 HCP but still worthy of a game try in spades. When partner produces . . .

♠ KQ
♡ Q875
◇ 6543
♣ 432

. . . you will have scored a goal because partner will have no hesitation in accepting your invitation to 4♡.

TRIAL BIDS
TREATMENT SUMMARY

REQUIREMENTS FOR A LONG-SUIT TRIAL BID

1. The **opener** should have a 5-card *major*.

2. The **opener** should have 16-18 HCP. Feel free to upgrade some 15-counts when you have some extra shape.

3. The trial suit should contain three or more cards.

4. With a choice of two suits, use the cheaper one for the trial bid. This gives the responder room to make a re-try in another suit which may have an important influence on game prospects.

5. A trial bid initiated by the **responder,** whose *major* suit has been supported, requires 10-12 HCP. In this situation, **responder's** trump suit might only be a 4-carder.

6. A trial-bid sequence that stems from an **overcall** might be made with a comparatively weak hand in terms of high-card points. As per usual, distribution will be the key factor in determining whether you should take this route.

7. The trial suit will normally contain at least two losers unless it is a prelude to a slam try. Consider this constructive sequence: $1\heartsuit - 2\heartsuit - 3\clubsuit - 3\heartsuit - 4\heartsuit$. The game try was rejected and yet the asker marched on to game regardless. What message does that convey? A *very* strong hand that has slam prospects. The second suit on these occasions is often a 5-carder headed by at least one top honour:

e.g.
      ♠ A Q
      ♡ K Q 9 8 7
      ◇ A
      ♣ A 8 7 6 5

TRIAL BIDS
TREATMENT SUMMARY CONTINUED

RESPONSES TO THE GAME TRY

1. Bid game with *any* maximum i.e. 8 or 9 if partner has opened, and 14 or 15 if you have opened.

2. Bid game with help in the trial suit even if minimum. 'Help' suggests no more than two losers so includes an ace, a king, a singleton, a void, a doubleton, and some queen combinations too.

3. If, as responder, you are maximum, and also hold a first round control in the trial suit, you should cue-bid this suit *en route* to game.

4. With a borderline decision the responder can make a re-try in another suit if it is below three of the agreed trump suit. Essentially 'passing the buck', this re-try should be used to indicate positive features rather than a singleton or void.

In each example, your partner opens 1♡ which you raise to 2♡.
Partner makes a trial bid of 3♣. How do you respond?

1. ♠ x x x x   Bid 4♡.
   ♡ J x x x   Minimum points but you have help in clubs.
   ◊ K Q x x   Accept the game try with 0, 1 or 2 losers
   ♣ x   by going straight there!

2. ♠ x x x   Bid 3♡.
   ♡ J x x x   Minimum points but no help in clubs.
   ◊ K Q x   Return to three of the trump suit with a
   ♣ x x x   minimum and no help.

3. ♠ x x x   Bid 4♡.
   ♡ A K J x   Maximum points.
   ◊ x x x   Accept the game try with any maximum
   ♣ x x x   – 8 or 9 HCP – by bidding it yourself.

4. ♠ x x   Bid 3◊.
   ♡ J x x x   Re-try. Tell partner about your diamond
   ◊ K Q J x   values. You may be minimum without help
   ♣ x x x   in the suit requested but it's still worth
                  showing goodies in another suit below
                  three of your agreed suit.

5. ♠ x x x   Bid 4♣.
   ♡ K J x x   Maximum points and a control in clubs.
   ◊ J x x x   Cue-bid the trial suit with first round control
   ♣ A x   *and* a maximum.

Trial Bids

GENERAL PRINCIPLES AND DISCUSSION POINTS

1. A long-suit trial bid must contain at least three cards. A holding of x-x-x is quite acceptable.

2. Responder accepts the try with any maximum within the context of the auction.

3. Responder accepts the game-try with 'help' in the trial suit even if minimum for the bidding.

4. Trial bids should not normally be made with balanced hands without five trumps but may, perforce, house those awkward 4-4-4-1 shapes.

5. A re-raise to the three level is purely pre-emptive e.g. 1♡ – 2♡ – 3♡. Responder is requested to pass whatever his strength or distribution.

6. If you want to make a game try when your hand is balanced with four trumps, the best approach is to rebid a natural 2NT showing 17-18 HCP. This also invites responder to select the best strain. In much the same way a 3NT rebid should not be viewed as a sign-off, rather it offers a choice of game contract based on the opener having a balanced hand.

7. When a *minor* suit has been supported, introducing a new suit is more useful as a *probe* for a no-trump contract. In this respect you will be *showing* a high-card feature in the suit mentioned. Use this as an *aide-mémoire:* mAjor = Asks; mInor = Informs.

8. Just for the record long-suit trial bids are not alertable.

1. *You open 1♡. Partner raises to 2♡. What do you rebid?*

Hand 1a	**Hand 1b**	**Hand 1c**
♠ J 5	♠ 7	♠ K 6 5 4
♡ A Q J 5 2	♡ A K Q 7 3	♡ K Q J 5 4
◇ A 7	◇ 8 7 4	◇ A Q
♣ A 4 3 2	♣ A Q J 5	♣ Q 2
16 HCP	16 HCP	17 HCP

Hand 1d	**Hand 1e**	**Hand 1f**
♠ 2	♠ Q J 6	♠ A K
♡ K J 7 6 5	♡ A K J 6	♡ K J 9 8 7
◇ A K J 7 6	◇ K J 6	◇ A
♣ A J	♣ Q J 2	♣ A 8 6 4 2
17 HCP	18 HCP	19 HCP

2. *You open 1♠. Partner raises to 2♠. What do you rebid?*

Hand 2a	**Hand 2b**	**Hand 2c**
♠ K Q J 7 6 5	♠ K Q J 7 6 5	♠ A Q J 7 6
♡ 8 7	♡ 8 7 4	♡ J
◇ Q J	◇ A 6	◇ 9 8 7 6
♣ K 5 4	♣ A Q	♣ A K J
12 HCP	16 HCP	16 HCP

Hand 2d	**Hand 2e**	**Hand 2f**
♠ A 8 7 5 3	♠ K Q 4 3 2	♠ J 8 6 3
♡ K J 7 5	♡ A Q	♡ A Q 2
◇ K Q	◇ 8 7 6	◇ K Q 6
♣ K J	♣ A K 3	♣ A K 3
17 HCP	18 HCP	19 HCP

Continued on next page – Answers on page 167

3. *Your partner opens 1♡ which you raise to 2♡.*
   What do you respond when partner rebids 2♠?

Hand 3a	**Hand 3b**	**Hand 3c**
♠ K J 6	♠ 7 6	♠ K 7 3
♡ Q 5 4 3	♡ Q 7 6 5	♡ K J 4 3
◇ 2	◇ K 5 4 3	◇ 5 4 3 2
♣ 9 8 7 6 5	♣ J 4 3	♣ 6 5
6 HCP	6 HCP	7 HCP

Hand 3d	**Hand 3e**	**Hand 3f**
♠ 8 7 6	♠ K 6 5	♠ 3 2
♡ A 8 7 4	♡ 9 8 7 6	♡ K 7 6 2
◇ 7 5 2	◇ J 8 7 6	◇ K Q J 6
♣ K 4 3	♣ A 2	♣ 9 8 7
7 HCP	8 HCP	9 HCP

4. *On the hands above, your partner opens 1♡ which you raise to 2♡.*
   What do you respond when partner rebids 3♣?

5. *On the hands above, your partner opens 1♡ which you raise to 2♡.*
   What do you respond when partner rebids 3◇?

6. *On the hands above, your partner opens 1♡ which you raise to 2♡.*
   What do you respond when partner rebids 3♡?*

7. *On the hands above, your partner opens 1♡ which you raise to 2♡.*
   What do you respond when partner rebids 3NT?

Continued on next page – Answers on page 167

8. *Your partner opens 1♠ which you raise to 2♠.*
What do you respond when partner rebids 3♣?

Hand 8a	**Hand 8b**	**Hand 8c**
♠ 9 8 7 6	♠ A Q 3 2	♠ K 8 6 3
♡ 8	♡ 9 6 5	♡ A 6 5
◊ K Q J 5	◊ 6 5 4	◊ 7 5 4
♣ 6 5 4 3	♣ 6 5 4	♣ 7 6 2
6 HCP	6 HCP	7 HCP

Hand 8d	**Hand 8e**	**Hand 8f**
♠ J 7 6 5	♠ A 8 6 5	♠ Q 6 5 4
♡ K Q J	♡ 9 5	♡ Q J 6 5
◊ 5 4 3	◊ Q 7 4	◊ 3 2
♣ 5 4 3	♣ Q J 7 3	♣ A 4 3
7 HCP	9 HCP	9 HCP

9. *On the hands above, your partner opens 1♠ which you raise to 2♠.*
What do you respond when partner rebids 3◊?

10. *On the hands above, your partner opens 1♠ which you raise to 2♠.*
What do you respond when partner rebids 3♡?

11. *On the hands above, your partner opens 1♠ which you raise to 2♠.*
What do you respond when partner rebids 3♠?

12. *On the hands above, your partner opens 1♠ which you raise to 2♠.*
What do you respond when partner rebids 2NT?

Continued on next page – Answers on page 168

13. *Your partner opens 1♣ and raises your 1♠ response to 2♠.*
    What would you rebid as responder?

Hand 13a	**Hand 13b**	**Hand 13c**
♠ K J 7 6 5	♠ Q J 7 6	♠ J 6 5 4 2
♡ 8 7 6	♡ K J 6	♡ Q 3
◊ A Q 7	◊ Q J 5	◊ A 3
♣ 4 3	♣ J 7 5	♣ K J 7 5
10 HCP	11 HCP	11 HCP

Hand 13d	**Hand 13e**	**Hand 13f**
♠ A K 6 5 4	♠ K J 5 4	♠ K J 5 4
♡ 3	♡ A Q J	♡ K Q 2
◊ A 7 6 5 4	◊ 8 7 6 5	◊ K J 8
♣ 3 2	♣ J 8	♣ 4 3 2
11 HCP	12 HCP	13 HCP

14. *Your RHO opens 1◊ and you overcall 1♡ which partner raises to 2♡.*
    How do you continue?

Hand 14a	**Hand 14b**	**Hand 14c**
♠ J 9 7 6	♠ —	♠ Q 2
♡ K Q 7 6 5 2	♡ A J 8 6 4	♡ Q J 7 6 3
◊ A 2	◊ Q 6 5 4	◊ Q 2
♣ 3	♣ A 6 5 4	♣ K Q 3 2
10 HCP	11 HCP	12 HCP

Hand 14d	**Hand 14e**	**Hand 14f**
♠ 5 4	♠ A 2	♠ A 7
♡ A Q 6 5 4	♡ K 8 7 5 2	♡ A K 5 4 3 2
◊ 3	◊ J 7 6	◊ 5 4
♣ A Q J 9 8	♣ K Q 2	♣ Q 4 3
13 HCP	13 HCP	13 HCP

Answers on page 168

1a	1b	1c
3♣	3◇	2♠

1d	1e	1f
4♡	2NT	3♣

2a	2b	2c
3♠*	3♡	3◇

2d	2e	2f
3♡	3◇	3NT

3a	3b	3c
4♡	4♡	4♡

3d	3e	3f
3♡	4♡	4♡

4a	4b	4c
3♡	3♡	4♡

4d	4e	4f
4♡	4♣*	4♡

5a	5b	5c
4♡	4♡	3♡

5d	5e	5f
3♡	4♡	4♡

6a	6b	6c
Pass	Pass	Pass

6d	6e	6f
Pass	Pass	Pass

7a	7b	7c
4♡	4♡	4♡

7d	7e	7f
Pass	Pass	4♡

8a	8b	8c
3◇*	3♠	3♠

8d	8e	8f
3♠	4♠	4♣*

9a	9b	9c
4♠	3♠	3♠

9d	9e	9f
3♠	4♠	4♠

10a	10b	10c
4♠	3♠	4♠

10d	10e	10f
4♠	4♠	4♠

11a	11b	11c
Pass	Pass	Pass

11d	11e	11f
Pass	Pass	Pass

12a	12b	12c
3♠	Pass	Pass

12d	12e	12f
Pass	4♠	4♠

13a	13b	13c
3♡	2NT	3♣

13d	13e	13f
4♠	3◇	3NT

14a	14b	14c
2♠	3♣	Pass

14d	14e	14f
4♡	Pass	3♣

CHAPTER FOURTEEN

COMPETITIVE BIDDING OVER 1NT

It is impossible to overstate the importance of having good systemic partnership understandings after an opening bid of 1NT – whether or not it was your side who opened, and regardless of the strength of the 1NT opening bid.

Whatever the weather or time of day, this call rears its head frequently and sometimes relentlessly. Whenever intervention occurs you must be ready and able to do battle.

I have deliberately left this chapter until the end because it is a complex subject to address. It includes defence to transfers and even if you don't play transfers, you will need to know how to cope should your opponents use them.

Now, I'm not a gambler but I wouldn't mind betting that even some expert partnerships overlook discussion in this department. If you do happen to be one of those very good players who forget the necessity to make defensive agreements with their partner over 1NT, I hope you will welcome this section with open arms.

There is a lot to cover, so let's get on with the show.

COMPETITIVE BIDDING OVER 1NT

FIRST POSITION
AS THE 1NT OPENER

I'll come back to this section at the end. That was an easy start!

SECOND POSITION
1NT HAS BEEN OPENED ON YOUR RIGHT

1. DOUBLE

Penalty. 15+ HCP. Any shape within reason. You are on lead which is a big plus factor. Balanced hands with less than 15 HCP should be passed without question!

HOW THE TREATMENT WORKS

(1NT) – ?

1. ♠ A K
    ♡ K Q J 8 7 6
    ◊ Q 9 8
    ♣ 3 2

    15 HCP

    Dbl

2. ♠ Q 2
    ♡ Q 8 7
    ◊ J 6
    ♣ A K Q J 8 7

    15 HCP

    Dbl

3. ♠ Q J
    ♡ J 6 2
    ◊ K Q 6
    ♣ A K 8 6 4

    16 HCP

    Dbl

4. ♠ K J 6 2
    ♡ A J 8 4 3
    ◊ K
    ♣ A 7 6

    16 HCP

    Dbl

5. ♠ K Q 4 3
    ♡ A Q J 6
    ◊ J 6 5
    ♣ A 3

    17 HCP

    Dbl

6. ♠ A Q 7 3 2
    ♡ Q
    ◊ A J 4
    ♣ K Q J 4

    19 HCP

    Dbl

COMPETITIVE BIDDING OVER 1NT

SECOND POSITION
1NT HAS BEEN OPENED ON YOUR RIGHT
CONTINUED

2. SUIT OVERCALLS AT THE TWO LEVEL

Natural. 10-14 HCP. Promises either a 6+ suit or a minimum of
5-4 in distribution. Your 5-card suit should be good quality with
two honour cards.

HOW THE TREATMENT WORKS

(1NT) – ?

1. ♠ A Q J 9 8
   ♡ 3
   ◇ 8 6
   ♣ Q J 9 8 7

   10 HCP

   2♠

2. ♠ 3
   ♡ K Q 9 7 5 3
   ◇ A Q 4
   ♣ 7 6 5

   11 HCP

   2♡

3. ♠ K Q
   ♡ A 4
   ◇ J 7 6 5 4
   ♣ Q 4 3 2

   12 HCP

   Pass

4. ♠ K J 7
   ♡ Q J 6 5
   ◇ A J 2
   ♣ J 7 6

   13 HCP

   Pass

5. ♠ A K J 8 7 3
   ♡ 6 5
   ◇ A 4 3
   ♣ Q 2

   14 HCP

   2♠

6. ♠ A J 7 6
   ♡ K 3
   ◇ K Q J 8 3
   ♣ 7 5

   14 HCP

   2◇

COMPETITIVE BIDDING OVER 1NT

SECOND POSITION
1NT HAS BEEN OPENED ON YOUR RIGHT
CONTINUED

3. SUIT OVERCALLS AT THE THREE LEVEL

Natural and pre-emptive with playing strength, and usually a 7-card suit. Distributional features, suit quality and vulnerability are important aspects. Points are not. If you play 2♣ as conventional a 3♣ overcall can be relatively strong.

HOW THE TREATMENT WORKS

(1NT) – ?

1.	♠ QJ97654	2.	♠ J62	3.	♠ 9
	♡ K65		♡ AJ98765		♡ 6
	◊ J65		◊ Q2		◊ QJ65
	♣ —		♣ 5		♣ KQJ7542
	7 HCP		8 HCP		9 HCP
	3♠		3♡		3♣

4.	♠ 76	5.	♠ AQJ8765	6.	♠ J
	♡ 3		♡ Q6		♡ J5
	◊ KJ98765		◊ 43		◊ A9876543
	♣ KQ3		♣ 87		♣ KJ
	9 HCP		9 HCP		10 HCP
	3◊		3♠		3◊

4. CONVENTIONAL SUIT OVERCALLS

Landy is my favourite convention in defence to 1NT, as I expect you have already gathered after reading Chapter 4. In a nutshell, a 2♣* overcall shows at least 5-4 in the majors with opening bid values, i.e. 10-14 HCP (occasionally 15 HCP). Below are a few more examples.

HOW THE TREATMENT WORKS

(1NT) – ?

1. ♠ K J 7 6	2. ♠ A 8 6 5 4	3. ♠ K Q J 7 4
♡ A Q 5 4 3	♡ K Q J 5	♡ A J 7 3 2
◇ 2	◇ 6 5	◇ 2
♣ 9 8 7	♣ 7 5	♣ J 7
10 HCP	10 HCP	12 HCP
2♣*	2♣*	2♣*
4. ♠ Q 9 8 7	5. ♠ A 9 7 5 2	6. ♠ K 2
♡ K 7 5 3 2	♡ A 7 5 4 2	♡ Q J 6
◇ A K 3 2	◇ K 5	◇ A 4
♣ —	♣ Q	♣ K J 7 6 5 4
12 HCP	13 HCP	14 HCP
2♣*	2♣*	Pass

COMPETITIVE BIDDING OVER 1NT

SECOND POSITION
1NT HAS BEEN OPENED ON YOUR RIGHT
CONTINUED

5. THE 2NT OVERCALL

Most unusual – literally! Best played as a game-forcing two-suited hand unsuitable for making a penalty double. You will be at least 5-5 and yes, you can have both majors even if you play the Landy convention since a 2♣* bid can be passed.

HOW THE TREATMENT WORKS

(1NT) – ?

1.	♠ K Q J 8 7 3	2.	♠ 3	3.	♠ A K 5 4 3 2
	♡ K Q J 7 5 3		♡ A J 9 8 7 6		♡ 6
	◊ —		◊ —		◊ —
	♣ 5		♣ A K 8 7 6 5		♣ K Q J 9 5 3
	12 HCP		12 HCP		13 HCP
	2NT*		2NT*		2NT*

4.	♠ A K 8 7 6 5	5.	♠ —	6.	♠ A K J 6 5
	♡ A K 6 5 4 3		♡ A K Q J 9		♡ A
	◊ 4		◊ A Q J 8 7 6 3		◊ K Q 9 8 7 6
	♣ —		♣ 7		♣ 4
	14 HCP		17 HCP		17 HCP
	2NT*		2NT*		2NT*

COMPETITIVE BIDDING OVER 1NT

THIRD POSITION
YOUR PARTNER HAS OPENED 1NT
AND YOUR RHO HAS OVERCALLED

1. YOUR RIGHT-HAND OPPONENT DOUBLES

   a) Conventions such as Stayman and Transfers do not now apply. All bids at the two level are best played as natural and weak including a bid of 2♣* unless, by agreement, you want to employ a conventional escape mechanism to locate a better spot.

   b) Jumps to the three level are also natural and pre-emptive.

   c) REDOUBLE: with 9 or more high-card points you can return the favour! It's game if it makes, or your turn to extract a penalty if they run!

HOW THE TREATMENT WORKS

1NT – (Dbl) – ?

1.	♠ 432	2.	♠ 8753	3.	♠ 975432
	♡ 64		♡ 974		♡ 42
	◊ 432		◊ 652		◊ J54
	♣ 98765		♣ J63		♣ J2
	0 HCP		1 HCP		2 HCP
	2♣		Pass		2♠

4.	♠ Q65	5.	♠ 43	6.	♠ KJ4
	♡ J8653		♡ 65		♡ Q543
	◊ 763		◊ KJ98765		◊ Q86
	♣ 32		♣ 87		♣ J54
	3 HCP		4 HCP		9 HCP
	2♡		3◊		Redbl

COMPETITIVE BIDDING OVER 1NT

THIRD POSITION
YOUR PARTNER HAS OPENED 1NT
AND YOUR RHO HAS OVERCALLED
CONTINUED

2. **YOUR RHO OVERCALLS A SUIT AT THE TWO LEVEL**

   a) Competitive bids by you at the two level are natural and weak – still ostensibly anywhere in the 0-10 HCP zone – but logically you are likely to be at the upper end of the range now.

   b) A new minor suit at the three level is invitational, primarily to 3NT. It shows at least a 6-card suit and approximately 11 HCP.

   c) A new major introduced at the three level is game-forcing (13+ HCP) with a 5-card suit.

   d) A cue-bid of the opponent's suit is *'Staymanic'*. With game-forcing values and at least one 4-card major you can bring Stayman back to life after your right-hand opponent has overcalled.

   e) Why not *double* for penalties if you have 9 or more HCP and four good trumps? There's nothing quite like extracting a juicy penalty!

   f) You can also bid 2NT or 3NT with the appropriate number of points but you cannot check up on a stopper in the opponent's suit. When your partner opens 1NT, it is assumed he holds a stopper in every suit even though this is not a pre-requisite.

   g) Even if the opponent's overcall is conventional, a double suggests taking a penalty holding 9 or more high-card points, and asks partner to co-operate once the opponents have located their fit.

1NT – (2♣) – ?

1. ♠ K 6 5
   ♡ J 7 5 3
   ◊ J 7 5 3
   ♣ 4 3

   5 HCP

   Pass

2. ♠ K J 7 6 5 2
   ♡ 6 5
   ◊ 3 2
   ♣ J 6 3

   5 HCP

   2♠

3. ♠ 2
   ♡ Q 6 5 4 3
   ◊ K J 7 5 2
   ♣ 9 8

   6 HCP

   2♡

4. ♠ 7 2
   ♡ J 9 8 7
   ◊ K 4 3
   ♣ K Q 9 8

   9 HCP

   Dbl

5. ♠ K J 6
   ♡ A 7 6 2
   ◊ Q 4 3
   ♣ J 8 4

   11 HCP

   2NT

6. ♠ K Q 7 3
   ♡ K 2
   ◊ A J 8 7
   ♣ 5 4 3

   13 HCP

   3♣*

1NT – (2♡) – ?

7. ♠ A Q 2
   ♡ 6 5 4
   ◊ K Q 2
   ♣ 9 8 4 3

   11 HCP

   2NT

8, ♠ Q 8 6
   ♡ J 6
   ◊ K Q J 8 7 2
   ♣ Q 2

   11 HCP

   3◊

9. ♠ A J 8 7 4
   ♡ 9 8 3
   ◊ K J 7
   ♣ A 2

   13 HCP

   3♠

10. ♠ A Q J 5
    ♡ Q 3 2
    ◊ J 5
    ♣ K 9 8 4

    13 HCP

    3♡*

11. ♠ Q 3 2
    ♡ A Q J 5
    ◊ J 5
    ♣ K 9 8 4

    13 HCP

    Dbl

12. ♠ J 7 5
    ♡ J 6 5
    ◊ A Q 6 5 2
    ♣ A J

    13 HCP

    3NT

COMPETITIVE BIDDING OVER 1NT

FOURTH POSITION
1NT HAS BEEN OPENED ON YOUR LEFT

1. YOUR PARTNER HAS DOUBLED 1NT FOR PENALTIES

a) Pass if you have at least 5 HCP and your hand is relatively balanced.

b) Make a weak take-out at the two level with a hand that cannot stand defending 1NT doubled. This action does not guarantee a 5-card suit.

c) Jump to the three level if you want to force to game with a highly distributional collection.

d) Go directly to game if you know the best strain and feel that your score for this will outweigh any penalty you might glean from 1NT doubled.

e) Bid the opponent's suit should they remove 1NT doubled if you want to discover a major-suit fit. Yes, it's Staymanic again and game-forcing. It does *not* ask for a stopper in the suit bid by the opponents.

f) If RHO tries to escape the axe by running into a suit contract, you can always re-instate the double with a useful trump holding. You do not need a lot of points for this as partner has promised 15+.

g) There again you might prefer to compete by bidding your own suit, rather than doubling the opposition. Partner will not expect you to have many points to bid in this position so long as you don't make a jump bid, but you should have at least a 5-card suit.

h) You may find it useful to agree that if your RHO makes a weak take-out into a minor suit and you have some points but nothing obvious to bid, a 'Pass' *is forcing*. This treatment paves the way for taking a penalty when your partner is able to double with a good holding in their suit.

(1NT) – Dbl – (Pass) – ?

1. ♠ 87
   ♡ 98642
   ◇ 432
   ♣ 432

   0 HCP

   2♡

2. ♠ Q87542
   ♡ 3
   ◇ 872
   ♣ 542

   2 HCP

   2♠

3. ♠ 432
   ♡ Q873
   ◇ J92
   ♣ Q82

   5 HCP

   Pass

4. ♠ Q65
   ♡ J54
   ◇ J3
   ♣ K8653

   7 HCP

   Pass

5. ♠ K4
   ♡ KQ98765
   ◇ 75
   ♣ 54

   8 HCP

   4♡

6. ♠ AJ753
   ♡ J42
   ◇ Q2
   ♣ 872

   8 HCP

   Pass

(1NT) – Dbl – (2♣) – ?

7. ♠ KJ653
   ♡ 87
   ◇ 982
   ♣ 432

   4 HCP

   2♠

8. ♠ 654
   ♡ 876
   ◇ A43
   ♣ QJ98

   7 HCP

   Dbl

9. ♠ QJ5
   ♡ KQ3
   ◇ 8765
   ♣ 432

   8 HCP

   Pass*

10. ♠ AKJ432
    ♡ 65
    ◇ J54
    ♣ 98

    9 HCP

    4♠

11. ♠ 4
    ♡ KQ543
    ◇ QJ65
    ♣ J72

    9 HCP

    3♡

12. ♠ K876
    ♡ K876
    ◇ KJ65
    ♣ 3

    10 HCP

    3♣*

COMPETITIVE BIDDING OVER 1NT

FOURTH POSITION
1NT HAS BEEN OPENED ON YOUR LEFT CONTINUED

2. YOUR PARTNER BIDS A SUIT (NATURAL) OVER 1NT

The strength of your partner's hand should resemble an opening bid with similar qualifications to those of a simple overcall at the two level. Your responses, therefore, are also similar, remembering that you can raise with just 3-card support. A change of suit must also contain at least 5 cards and is best played as a one-round force. Other options include:

a) Pass with less than 10 HCP.

b) Invite to game with 10-12 HCP.

c) Bid or investigate game with 13+ HCP.

HOW THE TREATMENT WORKS

(1NT) – 2♠ – (Pass) – ?

1.	♠ J	2.	♠ Q76	3.	♠ 32
	♡ K752		♡ 8732		♡ QJ65
	◇ QJ542		◇ K53		◇ QJ3
	♣ Q53		♣ AJ6		♣ KQ72
	9 HCP		10 HCP		11 HCP
	Pass		3♠		2NT

4.	♠ 7	5.	♠ A98	6.	♠ 2
	♡ AJ9872		♡ KJ65		♡ AJ97
	◇ A43		◇ KQ3		◇ KJ63
	♣ K93		♣ 873		♣ AJ87
	12 HCP		13 HCP		14 HCP
	3♡		4♠		3NT

FOURTH POSITION
1NT HAS BEEN OPENED ON YOUR LEFT CONTINUED

3. YOUR PARTNER PASSES OVER 1NT AND YOUR R.H.O. MAKES A NATURAL WEAK TAKE-OUT AT THE TWO LEVEL.

   a) Double is for take-out of the suit called. Partner will initially expect you to have the classic hand type for this call, i.e. 4-4-4-1 and opening strength, but you also have to cater for the strong, balanced variety where you have been denied the opportunity to make a penalty double of 1NT.

   b) Suit bids are natural with opening bid values.

HOW THE TREATMENT WORKS

(1NT) – Pass – (2♡) – ?

1.	♠ A Q 7 5	2.	♠ K Q 9 8 5 3	3.	♠ 4 2		
	♡ 3		♡ K 7		♡ J 5		
	◊ K 7 5 3		◊ Q 5 2		◊ K J 4		
	♣ Q 9 8 3		♣ Q 3		♣ A K J 9 8 3		
	11 HCP		12 HCP		13 HCP		
	Dbl		2♠		3♣		
4.	♠ K J 9 8	5.	♠ K J 4	6.	♠ A K 5		
	♡ 6		♡ K Q 3		♡ Q 2		
	◊ A Q J 5 2		◊ Q 7 6 2		◊ A K Q 3 2		
	♣ K 5 2		♣ A J 4		♣ J 8 3		
	14 HCP		16 HCP		19 HCP		
	Dbl		Dbl		Dbl		

COMPETITIVE BIDDING OVER 1NT

FOURTH POSITION
1NT HAS BEEN OPENED ON YOUR LEFT CONTINUED

4. YOUR RIGHT-HAND OPPONENT MAKES A TRANSFER BID OR USES 2♣* STAYMAN.

    a) Double shows the suit that has just been called artificially. As you are inviting partner to compete (the double is not just lead-directing), you are expected to have at least a 5-card suit and overcalling values.

    b) If the opponents are playing transfers, you can bid their *real* suit as a take-out manoeuvre!

    c) If you have passed initially, an immediate double will always be purely lead-directing.

    d) Holding a strong, balanced hand you can pass for now knowing that you will get another chance to bid on the next round.

    e) Other suit overcalls are natural.

$(1NT) - Pass - (2\clubsuit^*) - ?$

1. ♠ A 2
   ♡ K J 9 8 7 6
   ◇ 4
   ♣ K J 7 4

   12 HCP

   2♡

2. ♠ K 8 6
   ♡ Q J 6 2
   ◇ K 5 3
   ♣ A 3 2

   13 HCP

   Pass

3. ♠ 7 6 5
   ♡ A 5 4
   ◇ 9 7
   ♣ A K Q 5 4

   13 HCP

   Dbl

4. ♠ K 2
   ♡ K J
   ◇ A Q J 7 6 3
   ♣ 7 6 5

   14 HCP

   2◇

5. ♠ A K J 8 7 5 4
   ♡ 4
   ◇ K Q J 6
   ♣ J

   15 HCP

   4♠

6. ♠ K Q 2
   ♡ K Q 3 2
   ◇ Q 6 5
   ♣ A 9 8

   16 HCP

   Pass

$(1NT) - Pass - (2\heartsuit^*) - ?$

7. ♠ K 5 4
   ♡ K Q J 7 6
   ◇ J 8 7 6
   ♣ 3

   10 HCP

   Dbl

8, ♠ J 8 7
   ♡ A Q 3 2
   ◇ K J 5
   ♣ 8 7 2

   11 HCP

   Pass

9. ♠ —
   ♡ A J 9 7
   ◇ 9 8 7 6
   ♣ A K 7 6 5

   12 HCP

   2♠*

10. ♠ A Q 3
    ♡ A Q J 8 6 4
    ◇ 4 3
    ♣ 9 8

    13 HCP

    3♡

11. ♠ 3
    ♡ K 5
    ◇ A Q 2
    ♣ K Q 9 8 6 5 4

    14 HCP

    3♣

12. ♠ J 7 5
    ♡ A K Q J 6
    ◇ K Q
    ♣ Q 6 5

    18 HCP

    Dbl

COMPETITIVE BIDDING OVER 1NT
FIRST POSITION AS THE 1NT OPENER

(Got there at last!)

1. **YOUR PARTNER USES STAYMAN AND RHO DOUBLES**

   a) Bid your 4-card major if you have one.

   b) Bid 2◊ with 4 diamonds.

   c) Pass without 4 diamonds (you must now have clubs!).

   d) Re-double with a *very good club suit*.

HOW THE TREATMENT WORKS

You open 1NT and partner uses Stayman 2♣ which RHO doubles.
How would you respond?*

1.	♠ J 7 6	2.	♠ Q 3 2	3.	♠ K J 7 6
	♡ A Q 2		♡ J 7 5		♡ K 5 4 3
	◊ K J 6		◊ A 8 7 4		◊ Q J 6
	♣ J 8 7 6		♣ A J 6		♣ K 7
	12 HCP		12 HCP		13 HCP
	Pass		2◊		2♡

4.	♠ A Q J 6	5.	♠ K 6 2	6.	♠ K J
	♡ Q 7		♡ K J 5		♡ Q 3 2
	◊ A 4 3 2		◊ 7 6 5		◊ K Q J 6
	♣ 8 7 6		♣ A Q J 9		♣ Q 4 3 2
	13 HCP		14 HCP		14 HCP
	2♠		Redbl		2◊

COMPETITIVE BIDDING OVER 1NT

FIRST POSITION AS THE 1NT OPENER CONTINUED

2. YOUR PARTNER MAKES A TRANSFER BID AND RHO DOUBLES

   a) Pass with a doubleton in partner's suit.

   b) Complete the transfer with 3-card support and a minimum. (Don't forget you can still 'break' the transfer with four trumps.)

   c) Re-double with 3-card support and a maximum.

HOW THE TREATMENT WORKS

You open 1NT. Partner transfers with 2♡ which your RHO doubles. How do you respond?

1.	♠ A 5	2.	♠ J 7 6	3.	♠ K Q 8 6
	♡ Q J 7		♡ 5 4		♡ J 7 5
	◇ K 8 7 6		◇ A K J		◇ Q 8 7 3
	♣ Q 7 5 2		♣ K 8 7 5 4		♣ K Q
	12 HCP		12 HCP		13 HCP
	Pass		2♠		3♠*

4.	♠ 6 5 4	5.	♠ K Q	6.	♠ Q 7 6
	♡ A J 7 6		♡ K 5 3		♡ A 6 3
	◇ K Q 2		◇ 9 8 7 6 5		◇ K 6 3
	♣ K 9 7		♣ A Q 6		♣ A J 7 5
	13 HCP		14 HCP		14 HCP
	2♠		Pass		Redbl

GENERAL PRINCIPLES
AND DISCUSSION POINTS

I think I've covered everything you need to know to become a budding expert and as for . . .

LEARNING BY EXAMPLES

. . . surely by now you've had enough examples!

SECTION FOUR

ETIQUETTE

ETIQUETTE

HOW ALERT ARE YOU?

HOW TO ALERT

YOUR PARTNER MAKES AN ARTIFICIAL CALL

e.g. Opens 2♣* to show 23+ HCP any shape;

or: Responds 2♣* (Stayman convention) to your 1NT opening bid;

or: Bids 4NT* (Blackwood convention) to ask for aces.

1. As the partner of the person making an artificial call, you must alert both of your opponents to the fact that the call is not natural.

2. You must make this alert before your RHO has bid.

3. If you are using bidding boxes, remove the alert card from the box and show it to both of your opponents. In the absence of an alert card, you may call 'alert' or tap the table.

4. If an opponent wishes to know the meaning of the artificial bid during the auction, that player can only ask when it is their turn to call, and can only ask the player who has alerted.

   When the auction is completed the person on lead may ask questions about the bidding.

   Only after the opening lead has been made face down can the leader's partner ask questions.

5. It is not etiquette to ask the meaning of an artificial bid during the auction unless that player:

   a) Intends to bid, *or:*
   b) Feels the answer might influence his decision to bid.

HOW TO MAKE A 'STOP' BID

IF YOU ARE GOING TO MAKE A BID THAT SKIPS A LEVEL OF BIDDING, YOU MUST FIRST DISPLAY THE 'STOP' CARD *OR*, IN THE ABSENCE OF A 'STOP' CARD, JUST SAY 'STOP' or 'SKIP'.

It does not matter whether the call is natural or artificial:

e.g. Open 2♣* (23+ HCP):	STOP 2♣
e.g. Open with a pre-empt at the 3 level:	STOP 3◇
e.g. Jump to 4NT to ask for aces: 1♠ – 4NT*	STOP 4NT
e.g. Make a jump-shift response: 1◇ – 2♡	STOP 2♡
e.g. Make a jump overcall: (1♡) – 2♠	STOP 2♠

1. Place the 'Stop' card on the table (or say 'Stop!') and then make your 'Skip' bid.

2. Your LHO must then wait ten seconds before making a bid. In this respect it is customary for LHO to await the removal of the 'STOP' card which should, therefore, be picked up after ten seconds.

3. After a 'skip' bid has been made, the next player to call should pause for those ten seconds even if the bid they are going to make is obvious.

A jump-bid during the auction *can* cause a problem to the player next to speak. The pause is designed to save any embarrassment to a player who may not be able to make a quick enough decision about their next bid without indicating this difficulty to *his/her* partner.

By pausing, the tempo of the auction can be maintained without any unethical overtones.